P9-DCJ-898
LIBRARY

Alvin Toffler

McGraw-Hill Book Company

New York St. Louis San Francisco
Hamburg Mexico Toronto

By the Same Author

THE CULTURE CONSUMERS

FUTURE SHOCK

THE ECO-SPASM REPORT

THE THIRD WAVE

PREVIEWS & PREMISES

THE SCHOOLHOUSE IN THE CITY (EDITOR)

LEARNING FOR TOMORROW (EDITOR)

THE FUTURISTS (EDITOR)

3 4 5 6 7 8 9 DOCDOC 8 7 6 5 4

ISBN 0-07-064966-9

LIBRARY OF CONGRESS CATALOGING IN PUBLICATION DATA

Toffler, Alvin.
The adaptive corporation.
Bibliography: p.
Includes index.
1. American Telephone and Telegraph Company.
2. Corporations—United States. 3. Industrial management—United States.
I. Shapiro, Marilyn. II. Title.
HE8846.A55T64 1985 384.6'065"73 84-7181
ISBN 0-07-064966-9

Book design by JUDY ALLAN

ACKNOWLEDGMENT
The original report, entitled "Social Dynamics and the Bell System," beginning on page 25 of this volume and continued in the sections designated by the word "Report," was prepared with the assistance of Marilyn Shapiro, Research Associate.

For Heidi

Contents

Prologue

The Museum of Corporate Dinosaurs

This is a little book for those who intend to survive—for managers prepared to initiate drastic change. It is about every company faced with the need to rethink its goals and restructure itself.

Some firms are already beyond rescue; they are organizational dinosaurs. These are non-adaptive corporations, many of which will disappear between now and the not-too-distant turn of the century. Companies with household names and famous products; companies with assets in the billions; companies with tens, even hundreds of thousands of employees; companies with enviable reputations on Wall Street and seemingly unassailable positions in their markets—all are at risk.

For many of these firms 1955–70 were years of almost uninterrupted, straight-line growth in an equilibrial environment. In such a period, the formula for adaptation is relatively simple. Managers look smart—indeed, they very often *are* smart—if they simply do "more of the same."

Since then this straight-line strategy has become a blueprint for corporate disaster. The reason is simple: instead of being routine and predictable, the corporate environment has grown increasingly unstable, accelerative, and revolutionary. Under such conditions, all organizations become extremely vulnerable to outside forces or pressures. And managers must learn to cope with non-linear forces—i.e., situations in which small inputs can trigger vast results and *vice versa*.

The adaptive corporation, therefore, needs a new kind of leadership. It needs "managers of adaptation" equipped with a whole set of new, non-linear skills.

Instead of constructing permanent edifices, today's adaptive executives may have to *de-construct* their companies to maximize maneuverability. They must be experts not in bureaucracy, but in the coordination of ad-hocracy. They must adjust swiftly to immediate pressures—yet think in terms of long-range goals. And while in the past many managers could succeed by imitating another company's strategy or organizational model, today's leaders are forced to invent, not copy: there are no sure-fire strategies or models to copy.

Above all, the adaptive manager today must be capable of radical action—willing to think beyond the thinkable: to reconceptualize products, procedures, programs and purposes before crisis makes drastic change inescapable.

Warned of impending upheaval, most managers still pursue business-as-usual. Yet business-as-usual is dangerous in an environment that has become, for all practical purposes, permanently convulsive.

The international economy has been fundamentally (but only temporarily) restructured by the Arab oil embargo, the rise of Japan as a world-beating competitor, and the emergence of South Korea, Taiwan, Singapore, and Brazil as newly industrialized countries. The collapse of major banks and the mushrooming cloud of unregulated Eurodollars have destabilized the world banking system, and today's global debt crisis threatens to knock the remaining props out from under it. The condition of the world economy is anything but equilibrial.

Meanwhile, technological breakthroughs, deregulation, stagflation, plus volatile interest rates and other erratic forces subvert the strategic assumptions of even the best-run firms. Of course, one is tempted to ask, if companies have so far managed to survive all this, what else can happen to them?

The answer is: plenty.

Two decades ago, when I (and a very few others) warned that the end of Industrial civilization was in sight, it sounded melodramatic. Today, as the smokestacks crash around us, more and more sociologists, historians—and managers—are reaching the same conclusion.

One has to be blind to be unaware that something extraordinary is happening to our entire way of life. The swift spread of microprocessors . . . biotechnology . . . the electronicization of money . . . the convergence of computing and telecommunications . . . the creation of startling new materials . . . the move into outer space . . . artificial intelligence—all such technological advances are accompanied by equally important social, demographic and political changes. These run from the transformation of family life to the "graying" of the population in affluent countries (while median age plummets in the Third World), from conflict over transborder data flows to the global diffusion of lethal weaponry.

Are such events entirely random or unconnected? Or can we detect important patterns among them? I believe many of them are closely interrelated. That they reinforce one another. And that, taken together, they add up to nothing less than a mutation in our way of life. The changes facing us are at least as massive as those associated with the Industrial Revolution.

They threaten all our basic institutions, just as the Industrial Revolution threatened, and eventually transformed, all the institutions of feudal society. No wonder the rules of corporate survival are changing so rapidly.

When so great a wave of change crashes into the society and the economy, traditional managers, accustomed to operating in safer waters, are typically thrown overboard. The habits of a lifetime—the very habits that helped them succeed—now become counterproductive.

And the same is true for organizations. The very products,

procedures and organizational forms that helped them succeed in the past often prove their undoing. Indeed, the first rule of survival is clear: nothing is more dangerous than yesterday's success.

There was a time when a company's Tables of Organization (formal and informal) stayed put for long periods, even during periods of depression, war and economic growth. By the time a company had successfully transitioned from the one-man-rule of its founder to a many-layered hierarchy, it had also, most likely, bolted into place a permanent departmental structure. There were departments for manufacturing, marketing, sales, research and what-have-you. Line and staff were clearly delineated. Sub-organizations reporting to the top of the hierarchy provided fixed corporate services, such as legal, financial, and personnel. Serried ranks of vice presidents held it all together.

Once this iron framework was installed, the company might shrink or grow, according to its fortunes, but the basic elements of its structure usually held firm. Reorganizations—usually implemented when a new chief executive took over—were few and far between.

By 1970 when I wrote *Future Shock,* which dealt with adaptation to change, the frequency of corporate reorganization had increased. In that book I quoted a business consultant to the effect that "one major restructuring every two years is probably a conservative estimate of the current rate of organizational change among the largest industrial corporations."

Today the pace has grown hotter and the stakes bigger. Successive reorganizations not only occur more frequently. They cut deeper. In fact, we are witnessing the most rapid, complex and thoroughgoing corporate restructuring in modern history.

The press is filled with reports about this restructuring process. Thus *Industry Week* writes: "Hard times and the tough realities of an increasingly global economy are wiping clean the blackboards on which many companies have plotted their strategies. They realize that they must do something far more fundamental than revise numerical forecasts or modify their products and organizations."

Newsweek headlines an upheaval in General Motors, calling it "the most revolutionary change in the way GM runs its business since the company was restructured in the 1920s by organizational genius Alfred P. Sloan."

The Economist, in awkward prose, tells us that "Becoming corporate dinosaurs is the fate big oil is now struggling to avoid. . . . The companies are learning that to stay big in today's markets they have to think small. They are breaking up monolithic companies into separate profit centres."

At which point *Business Week* picks up the story: "The entire oil industry has come under growing pressure to reorganize its assets in fundamental ways . . . the large integrated companies that once seemed inviolable are no longer immune."

Giant oil firms divest themselves of familiar operations. Exxon spends vast sums on an unsuccessful attempt to enter the information industry. Arco invests in genetic research and seed production. Meanwhile, U.S. Steel goes *into* the oil business, and the steel industry as a whole struggles to scale down its plants and build "mini-mills."

Goodyear, a leader in the tire industry, buys a gas pipeline. At the same time, giant petrochemical firms struggle to leave the commodity business and become specialty producers. Hercules, the chemical company, now manufactures electronic controls for aircraft, and Ethyl Corporation finds itself in the insurance business.

Centralized companies race to decentralize, while a heavily decentralized Beatrice Foods reverses its long-standing policy of expansion through acquisition. Its Chief Executive Officer, James Dutt, announces candidly that, with 400 companies in its organization, the corporation has simply become "unmanageable."

Nowhere is the rate of restructure more frenzied than in finance, where banks are radically reconceptualizing their functions. As old barriers, definitions and legal restrictions collapse, brokerage houses overnight turn into banks; credit card companies become brokers; retailers transform themselves into insurance companies; corporate caterpillars try to moult into tigers in a frantic struggle for survival in the new environment.

And then, of course, there is what has been called "the most drastic discontinuity in the history of any major U.S. industry," or even "the largest corporate event in history"—the break-up of the biggest, and quite possibly the best, example of industrial organization in the world: the American Telephone and Telegraph Company.

In all Industrial history, whether in the U.S. or the world, no company has undergone a more complex and excruciating process of restructure. Because of this, there is much to be learned about adaptive behavior by looking at how this gigantic corporation began—some 15 years before the break-up—to reexamine its own premises and mission.

I was fortunate to be there at the very beginning. And that led to the unusual story behind this book.

Before I tell that story, however, it is essential to explain what this book is and what it is not.

This is *not* the story of the Bell break-up or an analysis of its effects. So many millions of words have already been written about that, it seems hardly worth adding yet another account at this time. The definitive story will not come for some years, after the less obvious consequences begin to show up.

So if you want a narrative account of the Bell divestiture—stop here.

The core of this book is, instead, a "secret" report that I wrote for the top decision-makers in what was then the world's largest private corporation. During all the years of debate and political and legal struggle over the fate of AT&T, this report remained proprietary. Now that the dust has begun to settle, AT&T has kindly allowed me to make it public.

Even a reader who is fairly familiar with the company and its recent reorganization can, I believe, find much here that has never previously been publicly reported or analyzed. Based in large measure on off-the-record, insider interviews, it sheds light on what was in the minds of AT&T's top management as they tried to cope with a rising sea of troubles.

Beyond mere diagnosis, however, the report called on AT&T to restructure itself radically and voluntarily. At a time when most of the company's top managers were still searching for "thinkable" options, its strategic recommendations were a striking example of "thinking the unthinkable."

Since then, of course, the unthinkable has happened. Nevertheless, much remains to be done as the new AT&T seeks to define itself, and some of the proposals made in this book are still no doubt capable of arousing hot debate. (One example is the proposal that AT&T basically reverse its corporate mission.) For these reasons, one can read this as a book *about* AT&T—post- as well as pre-break-up.

But there is a quite different way to read this book. For *The Adaptive Corporation* can also be seen as a case study. In this sense, it is not about AT&T alone. It is, in fact, a book on how to think about fundamental reorganization. While it focusses on AT&T, and AT&T is in many respects unique, the book raises questions which, I believe, are of paramount importance for any large organization in a period of rapid change.

It deals with the underlying assumptions of corporate strategy. It deals with the relationship of a corporation to its environment, including social and political factors. It deals with the effects of diversification on product line, administrative procedures, markets, technologies and competition. It then looks closely at innovation and how a rising curve of innovation affects products, people, and decision-making. It goes on to sketch the new economy and society emerging around us as the industrial age passes, and proposes new assumptions on which to base strategy.

The book directly addresses three key questions of organization: the "fit" of organization to the problems facing it; the changing nature of hierarchy; and the question of scale. In doing so, it touches on the role of vertical integration and alternatives to it. Finally, it devotes a great deal of attention to planning and to training.

All these questions are dealt with, using AT&T as the case in point. And once the analysis is complete, the book shows how new principles might have been applied to restructuring the telephone giant before it was compelled to change by government edict. The result is, in my judgment, directly relevant for managers in many industries.

It is also useful to know how and when *The Adaptive Corporation* was written. Some of the book is new—i.e., written since the break-up of the Bell System. This includes the present introduction, of course, and the running commentary that appears throughout.

The nucleus of the book, however, was written some years ago under remarkable circumstances.

It all began in 1968 when I received a wholly unexpected phone call from "195"—corporate headquarters of AT&T (then located at 195 Broadway in Manhattan). I had not yet completed writing *Future Shock* and my name was not well known. But I had served as an associate editor of *Fortune* and I had also, for *Horizon* magazine, written an article entitled *The Future as a Way of Life,* in which I called for greater attention to the long-range future.

Out of that first telephone call came what must surely be one of the choicest consulting assignments in recent memory. A vice president named Walter W. Straley invited me to spend several years studying the entire Bell System, as AT&T was then still known. I would have free access to every executive in the company, from the chairman on down, on a not-for-attribution basis. Protesting that I was neither an engineer nor an expert on telecommunications, I asked what it was he expected me to do. His answer struck at the central issue: corporate mission.

Straley explained to me that the Bell System (in these pages I will continue to use that term interchangeably with AT&T) had had a clear mission for over half a century. Its goal was to place a standard black telephone into every American home, and, beyond that, to provide any and all communications services to the nation. This mission was summed up in the phrase "Universal Service."

By the 1950s, however, most Americans already had phones, and Bell shifted from vertical to horizontal penetration of the market. It began to produce pink, green and white phones and other innovations. It broadened its product line—but it did not reconceptualize its mission.

Now, Straley said, with remarkable foresight, the Bell System was about to enter a wholly new phase. The entire communications system was about to be revolutionized by new technologies, new social attitudes, new government policies. What should AT&T's mission be in this next stage—and how might it reorganize itself to carry out a fundamentally new mission?

I was taken aback by the scope of what he proposed. I was being asked by the biggest company in the world to suggest a pathway into the future. My initial interest, however, was held in check by uncertainty. Exactly what would *my* mission entail? What actual output would I be expected to produce?

At this point in our discussions I received a reply that was so open-ended it flabbergasted me. It was a measure of the venturesomeness of both the man and his corporation, and it left me gasping. The answer was: "Make a movie. Write some magazine articles. Make a report to the board. Or do a book. You decide!"

That clinched the deal.

Here was a gigantic, tradition-encrusted company willing to look at its long-range problems, to challenge its own most fundamental assumptions as embodied in its mission, to entrust an outsider to make such a probe, and to let him decide even the form of presentation. The challenge was irresistible.

That began four years of intermittent research on the future of communications, on the role of innovation, on the often Byzantine inner workings of the Bell System, on the changes in the social and political environment that might impact on the company. I visited factories and laboratories. I interviewed the chairman and his principal officers. I met with engineers, lobbyists, accountants, planners, and, of course, with many people outside the company, from U.S. government officials to Japanese industrialists.

I also quickly tapped into an "underground" of Young Turks inside the company—men and women at all levels who were frustrated by what they saw as Bell's inadequate response to accelerating change. They sensed that AT&T's existing structure was becoming anachronistic in a world of computers and satellites. They saw increasing competition rising up to threaten not only AT&T's dominance but also the effectiveness of the nation's communications system.

Everywhere I received strong, often warm, support from them. Committed to the idea of service to the nation, as well as merely to a company, they opened up their thoughts, concerns and hopes to me.

In 1972 (having in the meantime published *Future Shock*) I finally sat down to put my reasoning and my recommendations in order. With the assistance of a researcher, Marilyn Shapiro, I reviewed every line of the material I had collected over the previous years. I then began to prepare a report that would integrate the best ideas I heard from insiders with my own by now strong views about Bell's future.

One thing became immediately clear. I was writing a report—in effect, a book—that would be a hot potato. It was critical. It was strategic. And it surely did not tell the company what so many of its highest officials wanted to hear.

For example, it was an article of almost theological conviction in the corporation that the operating companies, like New York Telephone or Northwestern Bell, had to be totally or almost totally owned by AT&T. It was heresy at that time to suggest, as I did, that the company "review . . . existing links between AT&T, itself, and the affiliates" and beyond that, that the company reduce its control over these subsidiaries by "opening a degree of ownership to the public."

The report's position on Western Electric, Bell's giant manufacturing subsidiary, was, if anything, even more blasphemous. For years the federal government had been demanding that AT&T divest itself of its manufacturing arm. The corporation, by contrast, insisted that such a move would be disastrous for the country—that Western must continue to be a part of a vertically integrated company. My report attacked both those positions and suggested, instead, that the company divest *part* of Western. It should, I said, sell off Western's routine manufacturing operations and retain only the high technology parts of the company that interfaced with the Bell Laboratories.

And if that wasn't sufficiently controversial, my report took Bell's traditional mission and stood it on its head. Instead of trying to provide all communications services to everyone, I argued, Bell should strip itself down in size and provide only "those products and services, *and only those,* that cannot be provided by other companies at equivalent levels of cost, quality, and social concern."

This was not a program for "dis-integration" of the Bell System, I argued, but "a conscious program for the dramatic *extension of integration* over a larger sphere," which I then went on to explain.

At this point I submitted my report unofficially to some of my friends in the company for their review. These were highly intelligent executives whose judgment and brains I had learned to trust. The initial responses were unpromising. Back came comments like "The tone will turn AT&T management off—overdramatic, apocalyptic, sensational."

Not everyone agreed with that harsh judgment. Nevertheless, I knew that much of Bell's top management would swallow hard when, and if, they read these recommendations.

On November 15, 1972, without altering either the tone or the message, I submitted *Social Dynamics and the Bell System* in, as I recall, ten bound copies. I had been led to expect an invitation to meet with the Board or the top management to present the report formally and to discuss it.

That invitation never came. Instead, there followed what sounded, to my ears, like an icy silence. AT&T, it appeared, would simply go about its own business—and I would go about mine. My phone, as it were, had been disconnected.

Years went by.

My reaction was a blend of disappointment and ironic amusement. The project had been personally rewarding. I not only had been paid for my efforts, but had learned an enormous amount about communications and industry. I had been given a chance to explore at first hand many issues that would be critical to business in the years ahead, from innovation to planning, government regulation, and the role of consumer and employee participation. So I shrugged, went on to other work, and assumed that *Social Dynamics and the Bell System* would spend the rest of eternity collecting dust.

But AT&T is not that kind of company. What I didn't know was that the report had taken on a phantom existence inside the firm. While it seemed unlikely that top management was going to react officially to it, Xerox copies began to circulate unofficially through management. It became a "samizdat" document—a piece of dissident literature.

Here is how Alvin von Auw, former vice president–assistant to the chairman of AT&T, and one of the men I worked with, has told the story in his own recent book, *Heritage & Destiny* (New York: Praeger Publishers, 1983):

"It is not the intention here to credit Mr. Toffler with more prescience than he would claim . . . ," but "Not unnaturally the question arises as to whether a more positive response to the Toffler recommendations . . . might not have saved the business enormous travail." Alas, writes von Auw, quoting no less an authority than Ecclesiastes, "For everything there is a season."

That season was soon to arrive. For in October 1975, three years after submission of the report, my wife and I found ourselves in Palm Beach, where I had been asked to speak at the board meeting of another Fortune 500 company. There our dinner partner turned out to be none other than John DeButts, then the chairman of AT&T. The moment of something-or-other had arrived.

DeButts, a big bear of a man, stuck out his hand, smiled

broadly, and brought us surprising news. The underground report had broken through to the surface. In fact, it was now being published in revised form and distributed widely in the company as a basis for policy discussion. What's more, the revised document told its readers:

"The original memorandum cannot be regarded as superficial—quite the opposite. . . ." The report contains "practical solutions to the problems of coping with what lies ahead. . . ."

I cite this not simply because it is pleasant to be stroked, even after the fact, but because it tells a lot about what it means to be an adaptive corporation. Here is a consultant's report that flies smack in the face of management orthodoxy. And here is the company telling its executives, in writing, that they ought to pay close attention to that report.

"Agree, Don't agree?" asks the preface to the revised document. "What is important is that you recognize the necessity, dictated by change, of the need for positive action in a planned direction. . . . In reading Toffler's Report, it is quick and easy to throw out the baby with the bath by failing to recognize which is which. It is our editorial point of view that the real 'baby' is the meticulous way in which he approached the recommendation given above. . . . It is of inestimable value for any Bell System Manager in preparing himself to cope with change to understand the path Toffler travelled in arriving at his conclusions. This is Toffler's main contribution to the thinking of the Bell System, functioning in the role of Mover and Shaker rather than as alchemist with the touchstone in hand."

How many other managements would be willing to circulate, even if belatedly, a document that so directly strikes at its own assumptions? If AT&T and its offspring survive the tremendous changes they have recently undergone, it will, at least in part, be because they recognized the value of fundamental mission reappraisal as a prelude to restructure.

Let me hasten to add the obvious: that, among all the forces combining to bring about the fundamental overhaul of the Bell System, I regard my strategic "game plan" as little more than a footnote. No company, let alone one as big as AT&T, changes because of a report. Only intellectual arrogance or self-puffery allows any consultant to claim the credit for basic restructuring of any large company.

Big organizations, as a rule, only change significantly when certain preconditions are met. First, there must be enormous external pressures. Second, there must be people inside who are strongly dissatisfied with the existing order. And third, there must be a coherent alternative embodied in a plan, a model, or a vision.

These may not be of equal weight, and they may not be sufficient, but they are necessary, and even a quick look suggests that all three were present in the case of AT&T.

External pressures may take many forms: intensified competition, government regulation or intervention, consumer, employee or environmentalist demands, customer and stockholder unhappiness, interruptions of supply, changes in taxation, interest rates, or currency ratios, and many others. (One can model such pressures and track their intensity.) In combination, these pressures must be so overwhelmingly powerful they make it impossible for the organization to carry out its own self-defined mission.

Internal pressures may arise because management fails to grasp new opportunities or because it is slow or clumsy in responding to external threats. Similarly, the organization may be stressed by insider politics, by struggles for succession, and other conflicts only tangentially related to the outside world. Often enough, an incoming CEO simply cannot operate as his or her predecessor did, or the new leader wants to plant his or her own political supporters in positions of influence, which may, in turn, necessitate organizational reshuffling.

Purely internal pressures, however, seldom bring a fundamental restructuring. For that to occur, it usually takes a powerful convergence of inside and outside factors, and there must be an internal "opposition" at work. I say opposition, in the political sense. This may very well be a loyal opposition, and it may not even conceive of itself as such. It may merely be a network of managers restive with the existing policies and structure, worried, frustrated by the company's failure to respond rapidly or imaginatively to the outside threats.

However, even when internal and external pressures converge, and a healthy opposition exists, fundamental change is still unlikely unless the insiders who want it can offer a coherent vision and strategy, a new proposed mission to replace the old one.

Unless there is a vision of a workable alternative to the existing structure, the resistance to change will usually triumph. Even if this plan or vision is ultimately rejected, it can still play a fundamental role in crystallizing the issues, mobilizing support for change, and accelerating adaptation.

Superficially, it might appear that the vast changes in AT&T were simply imposed by government. And, of course, the courts and the Federal Communications Commission and the Congress did compel the company to change. But to say that Bell was restructured solely because of government intervention is to overlook deeper causes. Indeed, a logical question to ask is why all three branches of the U.S. government felt called upon to intervene at all.

No one will ever untangle the multiple causes of the Bell break-up, and I doubt that many inside AT&T, even now, would agree with all that follows. But in any analysis of the situation, one thing is clear. Massive technological changes—many of them fed by Bell research—had begun to reshape American industry and society in the 1960s.

The computer, once a novelty, had become crucial to the entire economy, creating a voracious demand for new machine-to-machine communications. Satellites were opening totally new telecommunications possibilities. Communities were cabling up their television sets. And the entire society was becoming far more complex and diverse than it had been, thus increasing the demand for voice-to-voice, voice-to-machine and machine-to-voice communications as well.

Bell's traditional ideology as embodied in its mission held that it should provide for all the communications needs of the country. But these needs were suddenly exploding. Moreover, they were differentiating so rapidly that no one company, not even AT&T, could realistically dream of filling them. No matter how fast AT&T ran (and some critics charge that it ran slowly because it was protected against competition)—no matter how fast it ran, it could not satisfy the demand.

Nor did these demands come only from individual telephone subscribers. They came from companies racing to computerize. They came from the computer industry as well, a powerful new voice in the business community. What's more, as the new technologies opened fresh possibilities, new high-risk entrepreneurs moved in. Their numerous small, fast-moving, and maneuverable companies demanded entry into the new fields opened up, which often entailed a redefinition and limitation of AT&T's traditional rights. Together these groupings formed an amorphous, but growing and increasingly political constituency that pressured Uncle Sam to pressure AT&T.

AT&T's initial reaction was to lash out against this commercial-cum-political pressure, as it always had in the past. Its instinctive response was to circle the wagons and beat off the attackers by sheer force. Every resource—technological, commercial, legal, political—was, in fact, thrown into the breach, as the anti-Bell forces organized and lobbied and Bell fought back. It was a titanic struggle.

But there were internal divisions inside Bell, as well, even at the highest levels. At no time did I encounter anything resembling a disloyal opposition. To a man and woman, the executives I interviewed were strongly committed to the company, proud of its achievements, fiercely defensive with respect to outside attackers. However, many doubted that the company could ride out the storm unchanged. The notion that Bell could resist structural change was dubbed the "Fortress Bell" policy by some of its internal critics.

In 1949, as I've already suggested, the U.S. government, in a burst of antitrust zeal, had demanded that AT&T divest itself of Western Electric, its manufacturing arm. In 1956, AT&T struck a deal with the government: It would keep Western. But, in return, it would pledge itself to license its latest technologies to other companies (on terms that now seem ridiculously easy) and it would simultaneously agree to stay out of any unregulated business.

Now, in the late 1960s and early 70s, that bargain began to look less than ideal. As technology and the marketplace were revolutionized, many Bell executives began to wonder whether the 1956 deal would not ban the company forever from the vastly expanding markets based on new technology. Blindly defending its old order might merely succeed in freezing the company out of the future.

And some Bell executives even questioned whether the old mission of Universal Service was still appropriate. Doubts were spreading about the Holy Writ.

Naturally, I knew little of this when I arrived, but it is clear in retrospect, not only that farsighted people in the organization were starting to question fundamentals, but that those at the very top of the company were prepared to tolerate, and even fund, research by the opposition. My report was one example. Many others, less radical and perhaps more balanced in tone, were prepared in-house. Together, they helped management reconceptualize the company, its mission and its future.

This, then, is the background. In publishing my report in this volume today, I have resisted the temptation to rewrite those parts of it that cry out for revision with the benefit of a dozen years of hindsight. If this book has contemporary value, it is precisely because it is unretouched, unvarnished. One should not "doctor" an X-ray, or retrospectively rewrite the medical prescription based on it.

The basic text, therefore, remains exactly as it was submitted to Bell's managers. I have, however, added a short introductory comment at the head of each chapter. In these I have now and then cringed or chortled a bit, taking advantage of retrovision. But such remarks are clearly set off, so there can be no confusion about which parts were written in 1972 and which in 1984. (To make the distinction between new and old perfectly clear, I have put headings throughout the text. Wherever the word "Commentary" appears, the material that follows it is new; wherever the word "Report" appears, the subsequent material is from the original document.)

Finally, I have spoken much about the assumptions of management. It is only fair to say a few words about some of my own assumptions in thinking about organizational change and forecasting.

First, I assume that the structure of any company must be appropriate to its external environment—and not to just one dimension of that environment. In my judgment, too many business executives, economists and planners define the corporate environment in overly narrow economic terms. By contrast, I define the relevant environment to include a wide variety of political, social, cultural and other frequently ignored factors. (Because of its history as a regulated monopoly, no one at AT&T ever underrated the significance of politics. But even AT&T, in my opinion, underestimated the significance of social and cultural elements in its environment.) The corporate strategist must scan a wide horizon.

Second, I believe that the corporate environment has changed so swiftly and fundamentally in the past two decades that structures designed for success in an industrial environment are almost by definition inappropriate today. The task of the business leader or the corporate strategist is to identify obsolete structures and change them before they damage the operation.

Third, this means that many key beliefs about organization—ideas that "worked" in thc past—must be reexamined. A corporation is held together as much by shared management beliefs as by formal authority. If these beliefs are no longer valid, policies based on them will drive the organization in the wrong direction. Today it is essential to question basic notions about standardization, economies of scale, vertical integration, employee motivation, mass production and distribution, consumer preferences and hierarchy.

Fourth, I mistrust isolated trends, whether mini- or mega-. In a period of rapid change, strategic planning based on straight-line trend extrapolation is inherently treacherous. (Trends are either spotted too late, or they reverse themselves, or they convert into something qualitatively new.) This criticism of simple trend projection becomes doubly true if the trends are limited to economic and demographic factors. What is needed for planning is not a set of isolated trends, but multidimensional *models* that interrelate *forces*—technological, social, political, even cultural, along with the economic.

It is never possible for any author to enumerate all his or her assumptions. We all live in an architecture built of countless inferences based on an infinity of assumptions. But even these few are enough to suggest how I approached this study. Stating them up front should help in appraising the appraiser.

In conclusion, if these assumptions are correct, they help explain why the issues raised in *The Adaptive Corporation* apply not merely to AT&T, but to every large business organization trying to think its way out of approaching crisis.

The message of change is perfectly plain: companies will ruthlessly review their basic premises—and stand ready to jettison them—or they will become exhibits in the Museum of Corporate Dinosaurs.

A NOTE ON "SUPER-INDUSTRIALISM"

Putting a tag on the future is not as simple as it may sound.

Throughout this book the term "Super-Industrialism" is used to describe the emergent high technology society. I coined this word in *Future Shock,* published in 1970. And I used it again when I wrote *Social Dynamics and the Bell System,* the report that forms the core of this book.

Over the years, however, I found that some readers had leaped to the conclusion that a Super-Industrial society is merely a scaled-up version of the traditional industrial mass society—the smokestack world writ large. Nothing could be more off the mark.

For this and other reasons, I dropped the word "Super-Industrialism" in my more recent works, *The Third Wave* and *Previews & Premises,* and shifted to a different terminology. Setting today's dizzying changes into historical perspective, I labeled the agricultural revolution that began ten millenia ago the "First Wave" of historical change. The industrial revolution which spread smokestack society around the world, I termed the "Second Wave." Today's rapid and massive changes I see as a "Third Wave" that is creating a wholly new civilization based on high technology, information, and new ways of organizing for economic purposes.

Because I wanted the Bell report to appear absolutely verbatim, I have retained its original terminology. For practical purposes, although there are certain differences that may be of interest to scholars, general readers who have read several of my books may regard the terms "Super-Industrialism" and "Third Wave society" as loosely interchangeable.

Part 1

Yesterday's Assumptions

Chapter 1

Introduction

COMMENTARY:

An invisible line divides all managers today. It cuts across rank and function to separate those who see today's economic and technological changes as incremental, bit-by-bit extensions of the Industrial Revolution from those who regard today's massive changes as truly radical. There are "incrementalist executives" and "radical executives."

One group assumes continuity; the other recognizes the growing importance of discontinuity.

One group tends to formulate straight-line strategies; the other thinks in non-linear terms.

One tends to define problems cleanly, treating each as it comes along, more or less in isolation from the others. The second group tends to define problems less neatly, but to see them in relationship to one another.

One is good at "thinkable" solutions to problems—a leadership style which may be adequate in periods of environmental stability. The other is open to "unthinkable" solutions—which may be necessary in periods of environmental turbulence.

The environment determines which particular skills are most needed at any moment. Unfortunately, an incremental executive often reaches the top at precisely the moment when an exploding environment demands the skills of the radical. The mismatch is often catastrophic.

In this opening chapter I tried to show why the situation facing AT&T called for radical, rather than merely reformist, action. I explained how AT&T's troubles fit into a much larger pattern of social and technological transformation. Not only was AT&T itself in trouble, many other industries and institutions were also being rocked by change.

Looking backward, it seems to me that, with some exceptions, most of the industries and institutions I cited are, if anything, in worse shape today than when the report was written. Can this be said of AT&T? It is too early to judge whether freeing itself of the constraints of the past and divesting itself of its most mature operations will necessarily pay off. I believe it will, but the verdict is not yet in.

If we can expect even more accelerated technological and social change in the decades immediately ahead, then other companies will soon confront choices as stark as those that faced the leadership of AT&T. And throughout industry we should expect to see the decline of the incrementalist and the rise of the radical manager.

REPORT:

Most serious students of the future agree that the United States will undergo deeper change in the next two decades than it has in the past two centuries. This represents a sharp challenge for American business. We are in the midst of creating a new kind of society. Having completed the transition from agriculture to Industrialism, the United States is now moving into a new stage of development: Super-Industrialism.

Super-Industrialism will be based on more advanced technology, on radically different organizational styles, new kinds of interpersonal relationships, new sexual and familial values, new ways of experiencing reality. This will mean a novel environment for business. In turn, this new environment will create a new-style corporation.

The task facing AT&T* is to define—and to become—a Super-Industrial enterprise.

It is not yet possible to blueprint the corporation of the future. But it is possible to analyze some of the forces that will shape it. Many of these forces are already at work within the Bell System and will grow stronger in the years immediately ahead. Indeed, the Bell System has already begun its own transformation into a Super-Industrial corporation. Only if these forces are taken into account in long-range planning, and, more important, in corporate goal-setting, can Bell successfully complete the transition from its present status as the largest and most successful corporation of the Industrial Age to an equally significant position in the Super-Industrial Age.

AT&T'S PROBLEMS FORM A PATTERN

As the largest corporation of the Industrial Age, AT&T bears more than its share of responsibilities and suffers from a heavy load of seemingly disconnected difficulties.

* The terms "AT&T" and "Bell System" will be used interchangeably. Where a distinction is needed, it will be specified.

On the one side, a host of competitive pressures are arising to challenge the corporation—MCI, Carterfone, CATV, proposals for domestic satellites, the emergence of IBM and other major communications-minded companies, all threaten to reduce the sphere of AT&T's influence.

From another direction come mounting consumerist pressures: lawsuits and public embarrassments that spring from service failures; the rise of "telephone consultants" and specialists to help organize countervailing forces against the corporation; campaigns for lower rates for special constituencies—computer users, educational organizations, senior citizens—and increasing regulatory resistance to rate increases.

From yet another direction come demands that the system employ more Blacks and hard-core unemployed, which, in turn, because of training problems, trigger further service failures and consumer dissatisfaction.

In Washington, Nicholas Johnson keeps up a steady drumroll of public criticism of AT&T, making a special and effective appeal to young people. From environmentalists come new pressures to prevent pollution and to recycle waste, sometimes defined as old telephone directories.

In New York and other cities, Bell System planners face rising community resistance to new service installations. Meanwhile, vandalism and even sabotage increase, causing irritation and expense to both company and consumer.

This catalog of ailments is, of course, no news to Bell managers, and strenuous efforts are being made to cope with the rising "sea of troubles." These efforts, however, are premised on a dangerous misconception: the problems tend to be seen—both by outsiders and by management—as patternless or unconnected, and therefore subject to independent remedies. This report will argue, instead, that many of the difficulties facing the Bell System are interconnected symptoms of a much larger disorder, and that they cannot, therefore, be effectively dealt with one at a time. There is a distinct pattern to them and an underlying cause. *Many of AT&T's most pressing problems arise from radical changes in the external environment of the company, and the difficulties of predicting or coping with these changes at the high speeds required.*

AT&T'S PROBLEMS ARE SYMPTOMS OF LARGER SOCIAL CHANGES

To gain perspective, it is necessary to step outside the corporate framework. When we do, we find a pattern of breakdown evident in major societal systems. This breakdown is frequently triggered by sharp shifts in the quantity and character of demand.

Universities. Caught in a financial crisis, the traditional higher education system can no longer provide all the varied services demanded of it. Demands for specialized educational services, for individualized instruction and new types of courses, have created heavy strains. Open enrollment and special Black programs have led to charges that "quality" is deteriorating (although quality is never well-defined). Many private colleges face bankruptcy, and, despite a lull in overt protest, consumers—in this case students—remain fundamentally dissatisfied with a system that has grown obsolete.

The Stock Market. The failure or near-failure of major brokerage houses underscores the inability of the system to deal with rapid, largely unpredicted, up- and down-swings in demand. When stock market volume was high, brokers, mutual funds and other companies fell so far behind in their paper work that they could literally no longer cope—even with the aid of computers. When the market fell rapidly, they could not contract in time.

Railroads. The collapse of Penn-Central, the disintegration of commuter service, dramatize the plight of the entire transportation system. As common carriers, the railroads must fulfill their public service obligations, which means that they cannot control demand. Given the web of restrictions and competitive pressures under which they operate, they also cannot meet demand.

Cities. In New York and other urban centers delivery systems for essential services are cracking under the strain. The education system is not meeting demand. The sanitation system is staggering. Health services are overloaded and deteriorating. Transportation—by subway, bus or car—is increasingly costly and near-impossible.

Similar stresses are evident outside the U.S. as well. In London, a walkout of sanitation workers threatened to dump half-a-billion tons of raw sewage into the water supply. Garbage piled up in the streets and a power walkout led to brownouts. Paris, Tokyo and other centers are suffering similar problems.

One could similarly document the difficulties of the airlines, the post office, the welfare system, the electric utilities, *et cetera ad infinitum.*

Faced with these evidences of systemic breakdown, is it sensible to think of AT&T's problems as accidental or peculiarly its own? *AT&T's difficulties can only be understood if they are recognized to be part of a much larger phenomenon. This phenomenon is nothing less than the break-up of the Industrial order and the emergence of a new, Super-Industrial order.*

AT&T'S CENTRAL ROLE IN THE SUPER-INDUSTRIAL REVOLUTION

AT&T cannot avoid a central role in the Super-Industrial Revolution. In fact, AT&T is one of the key forces *producing* this vast social upheaval.

First, AT&T is a key creator of the advanced technologies upon which the new Super-Industrial system is being built. By pumping new technologies into the Industrial system—the transistor, for example—it has vastly accelerated the general rate of change and contributed to *destabilizing* the system.

Second, AT&T is central to this revolution because it is in the information business. In the past, land, labor and capital were the key elements of production. Tomorrow—and in many industries tomorrow has already arrived—information will be the crucial ingredient. By making possible swift and massive flows of information in the society, AT&T is helping to bring the Super-Industrial system into being. AT&T is itself an agent of revolutionary change.

Third, AT&T plays a special role because it is more exposed to attack than almost any other major corporation. Its nerve ends literally reach into everyone's kitchen or office, and can be stimulated at will by anyone choosing to do so. The level of stimulation in the telephone network is largely determined by forces outside the control of the company, itself.

Finally, AT&T plays a special role simply because it is one of the world's largest corporations. Its fate in the next 10–20 years will affect millions of people. Its example could provide leadership for thousands of other companies in the U.S. and abroad. By contrast, the breakdown of AT&T for any reason, even its temporary failure, could create social and economic havoc. It could endanger the security of the United States and retard responsible technological development throughout the world.

For these reasons, it is essential that AT&T's managers recognize a new goal for the 10–20-year period ahead: *to transform the Bell System from its present Industrial form into a form more adapted to the emerging Super-Industrial system,* and to accomplish this with as little internal upheaval as possible, while continuing to provide basic communications services to the society at large.

To make this transition, new and improved systems of planing will be required. These, however, must be based on an incisive understanding of the social forces at work on the company, and a clear appreciation of the basic differences between Industrialism and Super-Industrialism.

Chapter 2

What Theodore Vail Knew (1885–1950)

COMMENTARY:

Every business has a belief system—and it is at least as important as its accounting system or its authority system.

When a society is hit by a wave of technological change, it is often forced to reexamine its beliefs. For example, birth control pills, computers, genetic screening, cable television—all these raise new questions involving parental responsibility, privacy, racism, pornography and a host of other matters. The society may find that certain long-held beliefs are simply irrelevant or out of date.

In the same way, a company may also find its belief system inappropriate to the new conditions.

But identifying obsolete corporate assumptions is difficult because the most important ones are the ideas least discussed. They seem so obvious, they are taken so for granted, that they form part of what might be called the corporate unconscious.

For this reason, I decided to "psych out" some of the basic beliefs which had helped make the Bell System a success. I discovered that many of these had been formulated for the company by Theodore Vail, the nearly forgotten organizational genius who first put AT&T on the business map at the turn of the century. Vail was a radical, rather than an incremental, manager. Drawing on what he knew about the emerging Industrial society, he questioned the assumptions of more traditional businessmen.

Vail's ideas eventually themselves became scriptural. Generations of Bell managers grew up on them and accepted them because they seemed too obvious for discussion. What's more, as a basis for decision, they worked. Bell was incredibly successful.

But by the time I was invited in, things were no longer working so well. It was time to question whether the Bell belief system was still an appropriate guide to action.

If it is not alert, any company can suddenly find itself with obsolete machines. But rusty ideas are even more dangerous than rusty machines. In today's high change environment, can any corporation remain truly adaptive if it is still operating on yesterday's beliefs?

REPORT:

AT&T is unquestionably one of the great corporations in history. Unlike the banking empires of the Middle Ages, however, or the great trading companies of the Mercantile Age, AT&T was born into the Industrial Age. Its enormous success sprang from a profound understanding of the social environment in which it had to operate. Theodore Vail and the other founders of the Bell System knew, whether intuitively or consciously, where the Industrial system was heading and what made it tick. Knowing this, they were able to shape AT&T into an institution perfectly adapted to its time and place.

Here are some of the things Vail "knew" or took for granted about the world he lived in:

• That most men want the same things out of life, and that for most of them economic success is the ultimate goal, so that the way to motivate them is through economic reward.

• That the bigger a company, the better, stronger and more profitable it would be.

• That labor, raw materials and capital, not land, are the primary factors of production.

• That the production of standardized goods and services is more efficient than one-by-one handcraft production in which each unit of output differs from the next.

• That the most efficient organization is a bureaucracy in which each sub-organization has a permanent, clearly defined role in a hierarchy—in effect, an organizational machine for the production of standardized decisions.

• That technological advance helps standardize production and brings "progress."

• That work, for most people, must be routine, repetitive and standardized.

This set of assumptions about how Industrial society worked made it possible for the men of Vail's generation to formulate realistic goals for the corporation, and to invent effective technologies and procedures for implementing these goals.

Thus, throughout the youth of the Bell System, the drive for standardization was dominant. For half a century, roughly 1900–1950, the prevailing motto of the company was "One policy, one system, universal service."[1] No statement could have more succinctly encapsulated the assumptions of the whole Vail era, and it led to a single, simple corporate goal: saturation of the market.[2]

Since even as late as 1940, fewer than 40 percent of American homes had telephones,[3] this was no small task. Putting a telephone—the same black telephone—into every American home was a goal that was not only clear and easy to comprehend, it was plausible. It was unarguably good. And it was morally energizing.

AT&T people thus knew what their mission was, and this mission, moreover, was perfectly consonant with the spirit of the times. It fit the Industrial environment. Other companies were trying to put the same automobile, the same refrigerator, or the same vacuum cleaner in every home. Henry Ford summed it up in the well-known quip in which, he said, it was possible to buy any color Ford, "as long as it was black."[4]

This goal of universal, standardized service had important operating implications. It implied, among other things, standardized procedures for manufacturing—and AT&T became identified with the supposedly scientific attempt to reduce each individual job to a standardized sequence of "most efficient" routines. A rigid division of labor was ideally suited to turning out millions of identical products, and AT&T learned how to chop jobs and responsibilities into ever finer divisions.

Pressures toward standardization operated outside manufacturing as well. Operators learned to employ rote phrases. The hierarchical flow of power from AT&T to the operating companies to the district office facilitated the establishment of uniform standards in all phases of operation—from manpower training and job specifications to equipment quality, billing procedures, and customer relations. From World War I on, almost all company trucks were painted a uniform, military-like olive drab color.[5] And since the corporation sold identical products and services throughout the country, a nationwide marketing style and strategy was adopted, emphasizing universal service and "the voice with a smile."[6]

It is important, therefore, to understand that standardization cuts deep. It is not only the final product that becomes standardized, but the methods for producing, distributing and servicing it, the actual work procedures and organizational forms.

Everywhere, in short, Bell managers conducted an intense search for more and more simple, routine procedures that could be quickly replicated throughout the system. And their success in finding and standardizing such procedures contributed significantly to the company's economic dominance in the Industrial Age.

By the end of the '40s, AT&T had annual operating revenues of $2.9 billion.[7] It employed more than half a million workers,[8] paid $21 million in annual dividends[9] to 830,000 shareholders,[10] accounted for the lion's share of the market for all communications services, and was, by any measure, one of the largest private corporations in the world.

Part 2

Destandardization

Chapter 3

The Pink Princess Policy (1950–1970)

COMMENTARY:

The growing diversity of American business and society since the mid-50s is one of the most important—and overlooked—factors affecting the U.S. economy.

AT&T rose to power in a mass society. It was a world of mass markets, uniform goods and services, and long production runs. By the 1950s suburban sameness and mass conformity (of which McCarthyism was a political reflection) characterized American life. By the 1960s, however, a new diversity of life style, opinion, dress, family structure and consumer need began to make its appearance.

Companies began to introduce more different types, sizes, colors and models, more varied services and procedures. Each company saw its own markets diversify. Marketers increasingly spoke of "segmentation." But few saw the connection between their own marketing patterns and the deeper changes occurring in American social, cultural and political structure.

In *Future Shock* in 1970, I analyzed this new diversity. In the Bell report, I asked what it meant for a company whose success had been based on maximum standardization. By introducing a greater variety of sizes, types, colors, models and services, a firm may respond to the increasing diversity of the market. But what happens inside the company?

While computerization reduces the cost of introducing diversity, little attention has been paid to the ways in which this change affects corporate organization and human relationships in the firm. AT&T began to feel these effects earlier than many other companies.

For this reason, I found it an excellent laboratory in which to observe the organizational changes traceable to market segmentation. In turn, the historic break-up of AT&T has seemed to me to be almost symbolic—a segmentation of organization that parallels the growing segmentation of society itself.

REPORT:

By the early 1950s Vail's goal of market saturation and universal service seemed almost within reach. Looking into the future, Bell management began to ask whether the time had not yet arrived for a change of direction, whether, in fact, the company needed a new goal.[11]

Many companies, having saturated the market for one product or service, invent new models, sizes, styles, colors, or additional services. They shift, as it were, from a policy of vertical market penetration to one of horizontal penetration. Within Bell, bit by bit, more by instinct than by meticulously reasoned strategy, a new "horizontal" policy emerged. The corporate goal of universal service was succeeded by a policy calling for a multiplication and diversification of services to the customer. The era of the pink Princess phone had arrived.

DESTANDARDIZATION OF OUTPUT

In 1954 AT&T introduced its first line of color telephones—eight different colors in all.[12] This was followed by the successive introduction of the Speakerphone, the wall telephone, and the Princess phone and other innovations.[13] Before long, many households began installing what were, in fact, custom home telephone systems—a white wall phone in the kitchen, a pink phone in the master bedroom, an extension in the basement, etc. And because the telephone handset was a rental item, customers were hardly reluctant to change the color and model of their instruments each time a room was repainted or an apartment redecorated (an increasingly frequent occurrence because of higher personal mobility rates and the expansion in the number of rental dwelling units). Even occupants of one-room apartments installed a wall telephone in the kitchenette and another handset in the sleeping alcove.

In the business sector, the introduction of the call director and other increasingly complex internal communications systems paralleled this diversification of home products. The multiplication of special requirements in the business market was vastly accelerated by the rapid growth of the computer industry. Until the late 1950s Bell's business remained voice-to-voice communication. Thereafter an increasing percentage of network use involved data transmission—man-to-machine, machine-to-man, and machine-to-machine. Thus, in addition to the increased variety of voice-to-voice services, Bell began to face demands for ever more refined and specialized data offerings. In the ten years 1958–68, for example, Bell produced 45 different types of Data-Phone data sets compatible with 200 varieties of business machines ranging from simple card readers to enormous computers.[14]

By 1970 the variety of output reached staggering proportions. AT&T today produces an estimated 250,000 different service offerings (no one knows the exact number), ranging from a special hook for a handset on a PBX system (at a customer cost of 25 cents per month) to individualized corporate communications systems like the one at Lockheed Aircraft which runs to $12 million per year.[15] Bell produces approximately 1,500 different kinds of telephones including handsets in six colors, panel phones, Touch-Tone phones, explosion-proof phones, special phones for the hard-of-hearing, underwater phones, etc.[16]

DESTANDARDIZATION OF PRODUCTION

At the same time that its consumer line became more differentiated or destandardized, Bell's underlying technology went through a parallel transformation. One after another, important innovations—many spawned at Bell Labs—altered the technological base of communications. Integrated circuits, thin-film technology, and thousands of lesser innovations vastly increased the capacity of the Bell network. But this came at the cost of tremendous variety in plant and production.

The Bell network capable of some 5 million billion possible interconnections is now composed of over a trillion components, and the number is rising rapidly.[17] Thus the recently installed L-4 cable system between Miami and Washington, D.C., will, when completed, comprise more than 10 billion components, whereas the "old" L-3 cable system contained "only" 1 million parts. But the increase in parts is not simply additive. It involves a vast multiplication of types of components as well.[18]

This same increasing variation is reflected even at the level of simple terminal equipment. Thus, according to the McKinsey report on Western Electric, "with the growing number of models, colors, and cord lengths for station equipment, the number of inventory items at all levels has had to increase."[19]

To create and assemble these more diverse components and products requires a corresponding step-up in the variety of plant and production processes. In the words of Dr. Hendrik W. Bode in his report on technical integration in the Bell System, the shift toward destandardization brings with it a "marked trend toward greater diversity in the kinds of equipment which go into the telephone plant and the manufacturing methods necessary to produce it."[20] Elsewhere he once more emphasizes that "the diversity . . . of the new processes" contrasts to the "'metal-bending' of the old days."[21]

But *the most significant corollary of these trends has been the shift from very long, to relatively short production runs.* As Dr. Bode notes: "[Yesterday's] product line seems elementary by today's standards. . . . The vast diversity of products which Western makes . . . [now ranges] from items made by the millions, like subscribers' sets, to items whose annual production is no more than a few dozen. . . ."[22]

According to a recent chief executive of Western Electric, "we make 8 to 9 million of the ordinary 500 telephone sets a year. If you count the difference in color and the difference in other types, we make about 1500 different kinds or variations of telephones. So the runs are really getting shorter when you give the customer wider choices."[23]

In 1968, for example, Western Electric classified fully three-quarters of the handsets manufactured in its Shreveport and Indianapolis plants (which together account for almost all of the System's handset production) as "specialty instruments or new models introduced in the past decade." Only one out of four handsets fell into the "general purpose dial phones" category. Instead of extremely long runs of "general purpose" units, it was limited to shorter runs of more varied models.[24]

More and more, the system is also based on unique, rather than mass produced, sub-assemblies. The new Electronic Switching Systems, which are needed to handle the incredibly diverse configurations of demand, are not mass produced, but crafted one by one. "Until we got into electronic switching we had only three major switching systems," says a former president of Western Electric. "Now," he says, "there are literally no two telephone exchanges exactly alike. Every one is tailor-made to the option that the community requires."[25] Notes another Western official: "Every switching machine is different . . . the busy hours are different, the number of lines are different, the calling characteristics are different, the coin boxes, all of them are different."[26]

While this was, of course, always true to some extent, there is a sharp difference between the new ESS equipment and the old Number 5 Crossbar. The ESS consists of so many more components, and can be configured in so many more ways, that it involves a much higher degree of tailoring.[27] It is predictable that, as communities themselves become more varied socially, ethnically, economically, etc., the units will become even more different from one another.

It is important to recognize that *the concept of shorter production runs applies with equal force to non-manufacturing operations as well.* As the number of different services and offerings increases, the company must invent new routines for dealing with them. But as the number of routines multiplies, there is a decrease in the number of times each routine is applied. Thus in administration, in customer service, in all the day-to-day business operations, more people are doing more different things, while there is a generalized decline in the repetitiousness of their decisions and transactions.

This helps account for the choking sense of complexity that has begun to pervade the Bell organization in the last decade, demanding far more sophisticated management and a change in the personality and skill characteristics of the people required by the system. Also required was a new business outlook—a willingness to discard some of the most cherished assumptions of the Industrial Age.

To summarize: *On the spectrum that ranges from standardized mass production at one end and one-of-a-kind custom production at the other, the entire Bell organization is subtly shifting its position. Instead of moving closer to Vail's ideal of maximum standardization, it is shifting further and further in the opposite direction.* In so doing, almost without being aware of it, the Bell System has begun its transformation into a Super-Industrial, as distinct from Industrial, corporation.

Chapter 4

The Super-Industrial Communications Market

COMMENTARY:

What happens when a company loses its dominance in an industry? Is this necessarily a sign of mismanagement or decay? What must be done?

Before attempting to answer such questions, it is first necessary to find out what has changed. Is the decline a result of superficial competitive moves that new machines or a clever marketing campaign can solve? Is the firm losing strength in an industry that is itself dying—or its position declining in a growth industry? Even more important: is the decline related to structural shifts in the society or economy over which no company has control? Until such questions are addressed, it is impossible to allocate responsibility or define a strategy for corporate survival.

In this chapter I contended that AT&T's troubles were, in fact, structural, and that they were related to the growing differentiation of American business and society. From the 1960s on, this growing diversity created an exploding demand for specialized communications services—a demand no one company, not even AT&T, could hope to meet.

By 1972, when I wrote this report, it was already apparent that Western Electric would "never again control as large a share" of the market for terminal equipment as it had in the past. Satellites, cable television, and computers—technologies essentially outside the control of AT&T—were transforming communications. Very simply, the scale and complexity of change dwarfed even the Bell System's considerable resources. What was happening to AT&T was part of the society's historical transition out of the Industrial Age.

If so, Bell's problems could not be explained away as the work of hostile legislators or regulators or unfair competitors or nasty consumers. They stemmed from far deeper causes.

The same, I think, is true for many companies today. Executives who blame foreign competition, or oil prices, or "lazy" workers, or government regulation may, in fact, be hiding, from themselves as well as others, the deeper, more structural reasons for their difficulty. And they may therefore be dramatically underestimating the adaptive changes needed for survival.

REPORT:

The policy decisions within the Bell System that produced this shift toward destandardization did not happen in a vacuum. Nor did they result from purely internal considerations. They must be seen as Bell management's response to tremendous outside pressures that were at work on other communications companies as well. In fact, if we study the evolution of the entire communications industry in the past 20 years, we are immediately struck by the parallelism: much of what was happening within Bell was also happening outside it. Change in the *internal* environment of the Bell System was directly connected with major changes in its immediate *external* environment—the communications industry.

In 1950 the communications industry in America had a relatively small number of corporate actors in it. The relationships of these companies to one another and to the government were simple and relatively durable. Within the industry each company had more or less clearly defined functions. And AT&T's dominant role was secure.

By 1970 the communications marketplace had fragmented so sharply, into so many companies, offering so many alternative services and products, arraying themselves into such complex temporary configurations, that it was almost impossible to draw a coherent picture of the industry. Several things were clear, however:

1. the number of companies was still increasing rapidly;
2. the number of different offerings was escalating even more rapidly;
3. the relationships between companies, competitive or otherwise, were multiplying exponentially;
4. the functional divisions among them were increasingly blurred;
5. and AT&T's dominance was being challenged.

DESTANDARDIZATION OF TERMINAL EQUIPMENT

In 1950, for all practical purposes, there was only a single important communications manufacturer in the U.S., Western Electric, with annual sales of $840 million.[28]

By the start of 1970, the market had exploded; Western's sales alone had soared to $4.8 billion, but it was no longer assured of the lion's share of the total market.[29] *The Wall Street Journal* reported the "intense competition for operational equipment is giving Western Electric one big headache. . . . The manufacturing arm of the Bell System will [not] have anywhere near its past growth rate."[30]

This upheaval in the terminal market can be attributed in part to the Carterfone decision which spawned a fast-growing terminal market fragmented into countless previously non-existent segments. Customers suddenly found the need for incredibly varied terminal equipment.

This destandardization of demand has led to a proliferation of manufacturers who have rushed to compete by offering equipment too specialized for Western to bother with. This point is confirmed by a senior West Coast AT&T executive who attributes the growth in the number of non-Bell "telephone consultants" to "the complex requirements of [the] business customer."[31] Notes the president of ITT's Communications Equipment and Systems Division: "The real advantage . . . is the custom-tailored communications we offer."[32]

ITT is, of course, only one of a host of eager entries into the marketplace. *The New York Times* reports, for example, that GTE and Stromberg-Carlson, not to mention foreign terminal manufacturers like Nippon Electric Corp., are preparing to compete for what is commonly regarded as a "virtually untapped" market.*[33]

* Interviews with the Chairman of the Board and top management of NEC in Tokyo confirm the impression that this competitor may prove to be a significant factor in the days to come.

The conversion of the terminal market from essentially homogeneous to extremely heterogeneous, from a reliance on a few kinds of widely used equipment to many kinds of equipment designed for small groups or even individuals, came at a time when Western Electric was heavily preoccupied.

Western was busy during these years unconsciously transforming itself from a mass-production-oriented organization to one more geared to Super-Industrial, one-of-a-kind assembly. But its very size and the heavy responsibilities placed on it by the Bell System—for new switching systems, for example—made it difficult to keep up with the exploding, and rapidly differentiating terminal market.

These developments suggest that although Western will no doubt continue to play a pivotal role in the industry in the future, and may, in fact, prove even more profitable than it has been in the past, it will never again control as large a share of the terminal market.

Acceptance of this new fact of life—a recognition that might have been bitterly resisted by Bell management a decade ago—is now widespread. It is reflected in the comment of one senior AT&T official: "We're now confronted with [a] . . . situation in which the needs of specialized markets for communications are growing so rapidly, the demands are so intense, that the question is raised as to whether the specialized needs of these markets should, if they can, be met by specialized communications enterprises."[34]

In the case of the terminal market, therefore, external pressures for destandardization were greater than Bell, by itself, could handle.

DESTANDARDIZATION OF TRANSMISSION FACILITIES

When AT&T launched Telstar, the first communications satellite, in 1962, many within the corporation generally assumed that it alone would ultimately control satellite communications, just as it had for years basically controlled the high frequency radio and underseas cables used for international communication. This assumption was rudely shattered by the formation of COMSAT. Indeed, the language of the Communications Satellite Act explicitly opened the door to competitive satellite ownership—and not merely for international, but for domestic service as well.[35]

Since then the political air has been filled with proposals for satellite systems or sub-networks that would, in effect, end-run the Bell network. RCA, General Telephone and Electronics and Fairchild Hiller, among others, have each filed applications with the FCC for permission to loft satellites of their own. COMSAT itself has proposed a domestic satellite system to serve the rapidly growing data transmission market.

Finally, in a particularly interesting proposal, MCI and Lockheed Missiles and Space Division have announced creation of an MCI–Lockheed Satellite Corporation and filed plans for yet another domestic satellite system to be built by 1975. With the federal government guaranteeing massive loans to Lockheed, the result of this plan might be a satellite system that is competitive with AT&T, yet indirectly subsidized by federal funds.[36]

On June 16, 1972, the FCC ratified a "multiple entry" policy for the domestic satellite market, with specific restraints on AT&T's participation, creating in addition potentially new competition for Bell's Long Lines market.[37] The eventual outcome of the FCC decision process still remains to be seen, but the directions of change are clear: no one company will control the sky, and a multiplicity of services and sub-networks are likely to be offered to the consumer.

On the ground, there is a parallel, perhaps even stronger, push to diversify or destandardize transmission facilities. This is particularly true in the data transmission market, which, by all estimates, will expand at extremely rapid rates in the years immediately ahead. In 1970 perhaps 80 percent of all data transmission moves through the Bell System, accounting for 3 percent of Bell revenues.[38] It has been estimated that by 1980 data transmission could account for as much as 50 percent of all Bell revenues. The more conservative estimates speak in terms of 10 percent.[39]

However, partly because of AT&T's difficulty in meeting the diverse needs of data transmission customers, the company faces intense competition, both as a common carrier and as an operator of private line communications systems. The data market, perhaps even more than the voice-to-voice market, is characterized by destandardized demand, calling for what are variously termed "a wide range of customized services," "special-service carriers," and "custom phone networks." In fact, the FCC based its decision on the MCI case on the basis that "the entrants would mainly be developing new, specialized markets rather than competing for existing business."[40]

Thus it seems highly likely that in the data transmission market AT&T will be vying with several competitive nationwide microwave systems. In the first 18 months after the FCC's MCI decision, according to *The New York Times,* "30 more companies have filed for permission to build nearly 2,000 microwave stations for various specialized offerings—ranging from the West Texas Microwave Company's plan for a $5.5 million link among the largest cities in Texas, to the Data Transmission Company's application to build a $375 million switched national network."[41] Ironically, as of 1970, MCI was already on the receiving end of competition from three firms for the West Coast markets: Southern Pacific RR, Microwave Service Co., and Sierra Microwave.[42]

While not all of these plans will be approved, and some may never materialize for other reasons, the basic fact remains: the data market demands increasingly varied or destandardized transmission facilities on the ground as well as in the sky.

This is why *it is a mistake to regard the emergence of these rival transmission systems as simple cream-skimming* made possible by a callous or hostile FCC. The appeal of MCI and many of the others lies not *only* in low rates based on AT&T's competitive disadvantage, but also on their ability to provide highly specialized services that Bell, for one reason or another, has been unable or reluctant to supply.[43]

Ironically, *the successes of the Vail era in building facilities for "universal service" must be now reexamined in the light of a communications market in which demand is increasingly fragmented into highly specialized sub-markets.*

Just as AT&T is handicapped in its competitive battle by the FCC's insistence on standardized rates in certain fields, so, too, is it handicapped in this new rivalry by its own standardizing traditions. Thus even if Bell were allowed to confront price competition fairly, it might still face considerable difficulty unless it could destandardize its offerings even more rapidly than it is already doing.

DESTANDARDIZATION OF MESSAGE ORIGINATION

Not only are the means for transmission and reception multiplying and differentiating, but, significantly, a parallel process is taking place in the field of message origination. The recent innovations in cable television and videocassette represent a forward leap in technology that may have a shattering impact on the great broadcasting networks and stations of today.

ABC, NBC and CBS, viewed as "producers," were built on the same assumptions that the Vail generation employed many years earlier in creating the Bell System. These assumptions point sharply toward centralization of production, and the networks, by linking up local stations, succeeded in centralizing—and "massifying"—production. They increased the size of audience for a given program and thus amortized production cost over a larger number of "units." Broadcasting, as we have known it, was thus based on a scarcity of channels and on the transmission of programs from a single central point to many points. Millions of viewers all see the same Johnny Carson show or the same news with Walter Cronkite. In effect, they receive standardized output.

Cable and videocassette, however, will have the effect of radically multiplying the number of message originators, decentralizing and, above all, destandardizing the output. More and more different messages will flow through the system, and small sub-groups of consumers, even individuals, will be served programming designed for their own specialized needs, tastes or interests.* Indeed, the very line between producer and consumer is blurred when, through the use of tape recorders, video recorders and wired communities, any individual or small group can produce his or their own programming. Even the terms "*mass* media" and "*broad*casting" will need revision.

This entire process is directly analogous to the generalized destandardization occurring in other parts of the communications market as the Super-Industrial communications picture begins to take shape.

Meanwhile, the accelerated growth of cable television, like the proliferation of satellites and microwave systems, is likely to further diversify AT&T's competition—especially in the rapidly expanding broadband market. The president of one major cable system succinctly stated the challenge in the December 1970 issue of *Communications News:* "I don't think it is easy or wise to ignore us any longer . . . we no longer think of ourselves as just a cable TV company but, rather, as part of a new breed . . . a broadband communications company. In fact, we see cable TV as the leading edge of the broadband revolution . . . or more precisely, evolution. We see it as only a beginning . . . one link

* Thus *The Wall Street Journal* observes that "cable TV should prove to be the best thing for advertisers since the invention of the sandwich board. When the systems become more advanced, ads can be beamed at small, specific audiences—every subscriber within walking distance of a certain delicatessen, for instance, or every subscriber in a high-income area or in a ghetto. Unlike on regular television or in mass magazines or newspapers, the advertisers wouldn't have to pay for sending their messages to everyone when they really wanted to reach just a specific group. Different messages could be sent to different groups at the same time."[44]

in a system that tomorrow will also utilize communications satellites and local distribution microwave . . . and, by the day after tomorrow may have progressed to heaven knows what other, newer form. . . . Thus, we are talking not merely about a national cable net but about a national broadband net of much greater flexibility and sophistication."[45]

The potential sophistication of the CATV system of the next decade is apparent in the announced intention of TelePrompter Corp. to join with Hughes Aircraft to build a microwave system and in filing an application for a domestic satellite system to be used as part of a cable transmission network which now encompasses 100 systems in 29 states.[46]

According to Dr. Peter C. Goldmark, former president of CBS Laboratories, such a link-up of cable and satellites could lead not merely to increased diversity in entertainment, but could provide federal, state and local agencies concerned with health, crime, education, welfare and similar functions with their own coast-to-coast or local channels.[47]

It is too early to estimate whether CATV will, in fact, develop two-way switching capacity or to what extent CATV broadband services will encroach on AT&T's broadband and Picturephone markets, not only for data transmission but for shopping, banking, entertainment and other residential services. However, there is every reason to believe that trends in the broadband communications market will parallel the diversification of competitive patterns in other communications fields as a whole.

The failure to see connections between these seemingly unrelated destandardizing processes lies at the heart of many of AT&T's long-term difficulties. For this all-encompassing pressure toward diversity is much bigger and more important than is at first apparent. *The fragmentation described above—in AT&T's products and services, in its internal organization and procedures, and in the communications marketplace as a whole—can only be properly understood when it is recognized to be a specialized example of a much larger revolutionary process.*

DESTANDARDIZATION OF THE SOCIAL CONTEXT

AT&T operates within a social context. Like a fish in a tank or a spaceman in his capsule, the company is totally dependent upon its environment. The communications marketplace, which AT&T executives study closely, is, however, only the most visible edge of the social environment. Ultimately, *what happens to AT&T is heavily dependent on changes in the wider society.*

Thus if we look outside the communications industry to trends in other industries, we are once again struck by the parallels. There is scarcely a business today that is not multiplying the types, models, brands, sizes and other variations in its product lines. The fashion industry offers only the most garish example. Instead of a single standard "look," there is now a fantastic variety of acceptable dress. Even in relatively conservative Britain, where white shirts used to dominate men's shirt production, a flashy diversity of colored shirts now account for 70 percent of the total. The "standard" white shirt now represents only 30 percent of the whole.[48]

Even in underclothes, where, presumably, fashion is less important, a former chain retailer states: "We used to sell a slip for $3.99 with such attributes as tailoring or lace and give that the big push, but now we try to impress them with broad assortments, having a wide selection of sizes, colors, and styles. Why? People no longer want to be told to buy a specific item—they want choice, a variety."[49]

In packaged goods, in gasolines, in convenience foods, in cigarettes, in home appliances, the same underlying process is taking place—a destandardization of output in response to rising consumer demands for variety.

In the auto industry, Ford, notwithstanding its founder's policy of standardization, today advertises its Mustang with the claim: "It's three different body styles, six different engines, and 55 different options that help make each Mustang as unique as the man who owns it."[50] Even the increase in options offered, however, is apparently insufficient, so that, increasingly, consumers—and especially young consumers—are "doctoring" their products or further customizing them. In California, where many consumer trends first become evident, a radical change has overtaken the automotive scene. Here is how one recent report describes California's by now "conventional" vehicular sights:

"Menacing chrome-plated 'chopper' bikes with upswept tailpipes and extended front ends . . . full-throated dune buggies, 'street rods' and street dragsters in a dozen shapes and a hundred colors—apricot, shell pink, Prussian blue, salmon, jubilee grape . . . Vans of every make—stock VW's, Fords, Chevies and even converted milk and mail trucks—painted in wild psychedelic colors . . . motorcades of precisely restored antique cars. . . ." And so forth.[51]

What we see here is a strong push toward individualization, reflecting a consumer belief that, as one writer puts it, "By God, I'm not like the other 20,000 in this development; I'm somebody."[52] This attempt to customize personal technology springs from the same impulse that leads young people to buy blue jeans and then tie-dye them or sew patches on them. And it is the exact parallel of the push toward antique or idiosyncratic telephones, which, in turn, mirrors the businessman's demand for increasingly specialized private line systems or hand-tailored PBX installations.

Even outside the ordinary consumer market, similar demands are growing for destandardization.

In education, there is a strong trend toward the "individualization of instruction." The introduction of "voucher plans" is under serious discussion as a way of breaking up the uniformity of school systems, and hence, of the services they provide. The creation of "free universities," "open schools" and the struggle by Black, Chicano or Puerto Rican groups for "community control" of local school systems are further evidences of the push toward destandardization.

In the mass media, we are witnessing the decline of what might be called the "mega-magazines"—the magazines that carry a standardized message to the largest number of readers. While *Look* and *The Saturday Evening Post* die, and *Life* barely hangs on, hundreds of new magazines burst into being—"mini-magazines" aimed at small, specialized audiences of surfers, private pilots, teenagers, hot rodders, retired people, organic farmers and the like. At the same time, a varied underground press crops up around the nation. This underground press itself is fragmented into specialized pages carrying even more specialized messages for Blacks, Jews, "video freaks" and other sub-groups.

The crack-up of the once relatively stable and homogeneous economic marketplace into ever more numerous and temporary miniature markets both reflects and deepens emotional, ethnic, religious, vocational, regional and age-related splits in our society.

We appear to be moving rapidly away from the "melting pot" concept of America—the notion that all deviations or differences must be subsumed into a homogenous "American Way of Life" and moving, instead, toward a system based on far greater social and cultural variety than ever before.

At its simplest level the fragmentation of our society can be measured by the increasingly refined division of labor. The U.S. government's latest *Dictionary of Occupational Titles* lists no fewer than 27,741 entries.[53]

At a less measurable, but equally important level, we witness the rapid emergence of new sub-cultures like hippies, motorcyclists, African-oriented Black groups, surfers and so on, each of these subscribing to values that conflict not only with the once-standard "Protestant Ethic" but with each others' as well. And we witness complex new cross-group influences, so that patterns of Black political action are quickly adopted—and altered—by Women's Lib or by Gay Power.

Thus, instead of the American population growing more and more uniform, in line with the predictions of the past 75 years, it has begun to grow more varied, diverse, and complex. And just as individuals increasingly seek to differentiate themselves, these sub-cultures seek to differentiate themselves, thus heightening, rather than suppressing their points of conflict with the surrounding sub-cultures. *Many of our problems of "law and order" spring precisely from the inability of existing constitutional and legal systems to deal with this new high order diversity*. Under this strong centrifugal pressure, what is cracking is not only "law" but, more important, the underlying "order."

This helps account for the mounting pressures to "decentralize" government through "revenue sharing," "neighborhood autonomy," etc. In New York, Mayor John Lindsay has put forward proposals for governmental decentralization and the creation of 62 community planning boards as a way to cope with the complexity. Peter Straus, president of WMCA Radio, and many others have seriously proposed the secession of New York City from New York State. As the fragmentation process continues, we shall, before long, hear proposals for the secession of boroughs, or parts of boroughs from the city.

Thus, in the consumer market, in education, in the media, in politics and in many other fields, the same strong pressures are apparent. These pressures toward destandardization, operating in different industries and spheres of action simultaneously, are an important part of the Super-Industrial Revolution. To understand how they will impact the Bell System, we must first trace them to their source. Why, in short, are the consumer marketplace and, more generally, the social system, moving toward greater variety?

THE SOURCES OF DESTANDARDIZATION

Several forces converged during recent years to create the drive toward destandardization. The most obvious of these has been the rise in U.S. living standards. Median male income in 1950 was $2,831.00. By 1969 it had risen to $7,659.00.[54]

The period 1950–70 thus saw the emergence of a very large number of American families with money that could be deployed for services, over and above elementary needs, for luxuries, and for the indulgence of relatively individualized wants.

When a population lives below or only slightly above the subsistence level, its pattern of needs is comparatively uniform. Food, clothing, shelter, basic medical needs, transportation to and from work, and simple communications needs, are universal concerns, and therefore can be produced on a standardized basis, taking advantage of long production runs and the classical economies of scale.

However, as affluence increases, the range of wants widens. The individual consumer, armed with significant sums of disposable cash or credit, begins to insist on goods or services tailored to his particular tastes. Markets segmentalize and an incredibly wide range of new services and products—from vacation clubs, luxury cars and widely diversified toiletries to mini-circulation magazines, fashions, clothing for special occasions, gourmet foods, psychiatric care and specialized surf boards—spring up and, so to speak, ride the wave of disposable money.

This radical change reflects the *shift from an economy geared to the provision of a few basic "gut" needs to one that concerns itself with supplying the endlessly diverse needs of the "psyche" as well.*

Education also contributed to the destandardization of wants. Because of rising education levels, consumers had a much wider knowledge of how other people, in other times and places, lived. They had, in effect, a diversity of behavioral models and a far greater sense of the possibilities open to them in a high affluence culture. The consumer imagination was further enriched by travel, which, in the last two decades brought millions of Americans into face-to-face contact with foreign styles, fashions, values and products. And, for those unable to travel, the communications media supplied vicarious images of alternative consumption patterns and life styles.

The combined effect of education, travel and communications, therefore, was to extend the range and variety of consumer demands. These tendencies were still further intensified by population increase. Between 1950 and 1970, U.S. population increased by approximately 50 million—a mass of humanity almost equal to the total present-day population of England or France.[55] It was as though an entire nation of aliens had been transplanted and resettled within our borders. This analogy is less far-fetched than it might seem at first glance, when we recall that the 50 million new Americans, the first generation to grow up in a communications-dense environment, a generation hammered at by extremely rapid change, proved to be significantly unlike their parents. This post-war generation—a nation within a nation—thus brought with it demands for still more varied, previously non-existent goods and services—styled to serve the so-called youth market.

All these factors, however, were probably less important than a revolutionary switch in the nature of technology itself.

Throughout the Industrial Age, *technology exerted a strong pressure toward standardization,* not merely of output, but of work and the people who performed it. *Now a new kind of technology is emerging that has quite the opposite effect. Put simply, while Industrial machines standardize, Super-Industrial machines destandardize.*

The best illustration of this new social "law" is a computer-based laser gun recently patented for use in the clothing industry. This device, developed by Hughes Aircraft Corp. for Genesco, Inc., the nation's biggest manufacturer and retailer of apparel, is a pure example of Super-Industrial technology and it stands in stark contrast to the industrial technology it is soon to replace.

Before the Industrial Revolution, men's shirts, for instance, were created, one at a time, by the handcraft process on a non-standardized basis. No two were identical. Each was tailored to fit a single, specific individual.

Industrialization brought mass production, and in the typical Industrial Age garment factory, a worker spread layer upon layer of cloth, one atop the other. He drew a pattern on the top layer, and then, with a power knife, cut around the edges of the pattern, thereby producing multiple identical cut-outs. Businessmen, steeped in the economics of the Industrial Age, tried to cut costs by providing the worker with a more powerful knife so that he could cut a greater number of identical components at the same time.

The new Super-Industrial technology—the computer-based laser gun—does not cut more layers of cloth at once. Instead, it cuts only one layer of cloth at a time—but it does it faster and cheaper than the power knife it replaces. This Super-Industrial tool thus does away with batch cutting altogether. According to Franklin M. Jarman, chairman of Genesco, it can actually "be programmed to fill an order for one garment economically." This innovation may eventually destroy the present system of standardized clothing styles, making possible a return to total destandardization—"custom tailoring"—on a super-technology level.[56]

In many other industries, similar developments are reducing the technological cost of product variation—to the point at which it may eventually be possible to turn out one-of-a-kind items for less money than it used to cost to turn out multiples.

This step-by-step development, from handcraft to mass production to a new, higher form of handcraft, is one of the keys to understanding the Super-Industrial economy.

What we see, therefore, is the coming together of two interrelated forces: first, a rapid destandardization of consumer wants; and second, a new technology that makes possible the ultimate in destandardization—custom production. Moreover, if we look at the forces pressing toward destandardization, we find that all of them, with the possible exception of population growth, are likely to intensify in the years immediately ahead. In short, these techno-social trends point to the emergence of a new social context for business and the need for a fresh set of corporate assumptions.

In the past, the company that knew how to standardize most effectively was able to beat out its competitors. In the future, the company that knows how to destandardize effectively may prove the victor. It will be running with the surf of change, exactly as Theodore Vail and his men did in an earlier, but quite different time.

Part 3

Rising Novelty Ratios

Chapter 5

The Management of Surprise

COMMENTARY:

No problem facing American business is more important or less understood than that of innovation. Even companies committed to high R&D expenditures have much to learn about the implications of that policy for the non-research parts of their organization.

If R&D results in a flow of new product, what does that do to the inner life of the company? And how does innovation relate to diversification of product line and organizational structure?

But innovation is not just a matter of products, or even of technologies. It is also a matter of people, and each company, regardless of size, must face the problem of "novelty." In this chapter I introduced what I still regard as a key concept for innovative management: the novelty ratio.

There are moments in the life cycle of a firm when it must cope with very high levels of novelty, and other times when the novelty level is low. In turn, this raises questions as to the type of leadership required in the firm. A low-novelty company may require incremental management; a high-novelty firm may need radical management. Alternatively, the same firm may need different styles of management at different stages of its life cycle.

The issue of novelty also has consequences for make-or-buy decisions and the issue of vertical integration. The novelty ratio helps explain why vertically integrated companies may be less maneuverable and adaptive in periods of rapid change than companies that are not vertically integrated.

Finally, I argue that many companies—not just AT&T—face rising levels of novelty in the external, as well as internal, environment. One example much on managers' minds when this was written was the consumer movement. While the consumer movement has lost some of its punch along with its novelty since 1972, and while some of the specifics I alluded to now seem to me to be dated, the general argument about rising levels of uncertainty in the environment is, I believe, more than ever correct. And that takes us to the central function of management: decision-making.

One of the strengths of the Bell System over the years was its ability to create an effective bureaucracy—to make decisions "by the book." But while relying on the book may be entirely appropriate in a familiar or stable environment, it may well be disastrous in a novel, fast-changing environment in which the problems are themselves novel and fast-changing.

Such problems frequently confound the linear manager, accustomed to straight-line solutions to straightforward problems. Which is why high novelty, whether inside or outside the firm, demands precisely the kind of executive skills that traditional bureaucracies crush.

REPORT:

AT&T is one of the most innovation-minded companies in America. Its contributions to science and technology will rank among the key achievements of our time. When measured as a percentage of Western Electric sales to the Bell System, AT&T spends over three times as much for research and development as the average American manufacturing company, and roughly twice as much as other concerns in the communications and electronic component fields.[57] In the 1960s Bell found itself increasingly engaged in introducing new products and services, rather than repetitively producing the old.

Despite this important shift, little is known about the hidden costs of innovation in the Bell System. These costs cannot be properly analyzed until management grasps the concept of the "novelty ratio."

The novelty ratio reflects the "newness" in a system. It is the ratio of new to old. For example, if a company sells a line consisting of one new product and nine old ones, we can speak of a novelty ratio of 1 : 9. We may define "new" to mean introduced within a given interval of time—say, five years. Thus a ratio of 1 : 9 would mean it had added only one new product to its line in the past five years.

As we shall see, the concept applies not merely to products, but to technology, plant, and even to the repertoire of routines or procedures used by a company. There are, to illustrate, a finite number of prescribed procedures for signing up a new telephone subscriber. As the number of alternative service offerings increases, so do the number of routines or sub-routines for the business representative to choose among. Some of these have been on the books for many years; others are very recent. We can speak of the novelty ratio of administrative procedures, therefore, as well as of technology and products.

There are moments in the life cycle of any company when its level of newness—its various novelty ratios—are very high.

In the Vail era, for example, almost everything that Bell did was done for the first time. The technology of telephony was new, organizational linkages and designs were created from scratch, company-government relationships were just being laid in place, work routines were developed *de novo*. After the initial decades, however, the newness that Bell managers had to deal with declined. Settled patterns or routines were established and Bell people were able to solve most of their problems by adhering to these routines.

In recent years, novelty ratios at AT&T have been rising—precipitously. Now AT&T is entering a new stage in its corporate life cycle. In this stage novelty ratios will not only continue to climb, but do so at a faster rate. This means deep changes in both the internal climate for decision-making, and in the external world the company will have to deal with. It will change the place of routine in the life of the corporation.

TWO KINDS OF INNOVATION

The fact that Bell today commits an unusually high proportion of its funds to R&D is not simply an expression of intellectual curiosity or of some "inner drive" to innovate. It is made necessary by overpowering economic considerations, each of which produces its own kind of innovation.

The push toward destandardization described earlier in this report forces the company to engage in what might be called *additive innovation*. To keep up with the demands of a fast-fragmenting marketplace, AT&T has had to add models, sizes, styles and service variations to its line. This has the effect of adding thousands of procedures to the already enormous repertoire of routines. In both cases, whether with respect to products or to procedures, the net result is augmentative. The new is added on to the old.

At the same time, the forced pace of technological change in communications, and in the economy generally, has compelled AT&T to engage increasingly in *substitutive innovation* as well.

This is the creation of new products, technologies, processes or procedures to take the place of, or eliminate, old ones.

Thus two very strong pressures—differentiation and technological change—both converged to raise novelty ratios in the Bell System in a relatively short span of time. The level of newness with which Bell people, from top management down to the lineman and the operator, must deal, has climbed dramatically.

NOVELTY RATIOS IN THE PRODUCT LINE

The elimination of certain older products and services and the addition of thousands of new ones is reflected in the fact that by the mid-60s Bell drew fully 43 percent of its sales revenues from products introduced in the previous five years. (The comparable figure for American industry generally was 20 percent.) It has been estimated, moreover, that today 65 percent of all Western Electric products are less than ten years old.[58] Turned around, this means that only about one out of every three Western products is an "old standby." Furthermore, even among these older products, only a few have remained completely unchanged during the decade. There are, in short, very few stable, fixed products to "anchor" the line.

Recent years have seen the introduction of everything from Centrex, direct overseas dialing, Data-Phone, and call directors to Picturephone. The introduction of Touch-Tone has been hailed in corporate documents because it opened the way to "wholly new services, including access to computer services and private data transmission." Card-dialers, new PBX systems, Trimline handsets, and literally thousands of others that are less obvious to the average consumer add to the overall picture.

This proliferation of new products and services, along with the relative absence of "anchor" products complicates decision-making for Bell people, creates anxiety about "what business we really are in,'' compels them continually to learn new procedures, forces them to devalue and discard painstakingly acquired older skills, and calls for both a new kind of employee and a new organizational style. Before we can analyze its implications, however, it is essential to see how this infusion of novelty into the product line has affected technology.

NOVELTY RATIOS IN TECHNOLOGY

It takes new machines and processes to produce new products. To raise the novelty ratio in a product line, it is usually necessary to increase the novelty ratio in technology as well.

While this may seem like an obvious statement, it has implications for the Bell System that do not apply to most other companies. First, most other companies, in introducing a new product, can rely on outside supplier firms to do much of their technological innovating for them. Such companies may pay a higher dollar price for the components or sub-assemblies they purchase, but the supplier bears the costs, *social* as well as economic, of keeping the technology up to date. AT&T, by contrast, because it does so much of the work intramurally, cannot depend upon suppliers to absorb the costs of technological innovation. It must continually renovate its own manufacturing facilities. Thus if there are few ''anchor'' products there are even fewer ''anchor'' technologies, and Bell is forced to raise the percentage of operating funds and managerial attention devoted to new, as distinct from old or familiar, technologies.

Frequently, the decision to introduce a new product burdens the company with the need to invent all the necessary manufacturing processes and materials as well. In the words of the Task Force on Communications Policy, ''products such as integrated circuits and undersea amplifiers have required the development of dozens of new materials, a vast array of new manufacturing techniques, and of production facilities that are radically different from those of the past.''[59]

Thus the Bell System in recent years has been compelled to develop new processes for hydrostatic metal forming, for needle bonding, for continuous copper casting, for growing crystal under high temperatures and pressures, for the manufacture of Stalpeth cable and thin film integrated circuits, and for the use of the laser in the manufacture of glass encapsulated resistors—to mention only a few.[60]

These new processes create what the Task Force calls "fundamental changes in the manufacturing environment . . . radical new approaches to the art of production."[61] They require not only new kinds of physical environments—surgically clean work locations, for example—but new kinds of personnel, new work arrangements, new interdisciplinary blends of skill, new interpersonal relationships. They demand a great deal of adaptation both from the company and from the people in it.

By opting for vertical integration, AT&T has made the newness of its product line directly dependent on the newness of its own manufacturing facilities. Every time it increases the novelty ratio in its product line, it must bring about a more or less corresponding hike in the novelty ratio of its production technology.

The second reason for this tight coupling has to do with the network. In a standard manufacturing company like General Motors, the introduction of a new model may require a good bit of technological tool-up—but GM is not generally required to extend or modify an existing network in order for customers to use the new product. *AT&T must not only design and make the new product, once having done so it must also modify the network to accept it*—exactly as though GM, each time it created a new automobile model, had to pave thousands of miles of technologically improved highway.

Thus we have witnessed a truly astonishing succession of innovations in network equipment to keep pace with the innovations in manufacture, and to make possible the use of the new products. In short-haul carrier equipment we have seen a step-by-step movement from the N-1 of the early 1950s to the ON-1, the ONK, the N-2 and the N-3, on to the T-1 and T-2 digital systems. This has been matched by the movement from L-3 to L-4 and now L-5 long-haul coaxial systems. In microwave this same relentless forward ratcheting is visible in the addition of the short-haul TJ, TL-l, TL-2 and TM, not to mention the TD-2, TH, TD-3, TD-2A, TD-2B and TH-3 long-haul systems.

Simultaneously, in switching we have seen a similar chain of innovations ranging from the DDD, CAMA, LAMA, ANI and Centrex to ESS No. 1-2W, ESS No. 1-4W, the 1A1 Concentrator, TSP, a multiplicity of PBX equipment, and the new ESS No. 2, along with TSPS and a variety of electronic modifications of crossbar switching.[62]

All in all, over a single five-year period, AT&T added more telephones and more kinds of telephones than the total number laid in place in the first 65 years of the company's existence, bringing more newness—a higher novelty ratio—into the company's technological base.[63] In light of this, it is not surprising that new products account for a higher percentage of Western Electric sales than is the case in any major American industry, from textile to transport, with the sole exception of aerospace.

By 1980 the Bell interstate network facilities will be four times its present size. This means that only one out of every four miles of wire, one out of every four switching nodes, one out of every four microwave towers for the interstate network will be ten years old or more. Three out of four components of the interstate network will be under ten years old, and a majority, perhaps, under five years old. In effect, AT&T will be managing a new network.[64]

The consequences of this, however, will be deeper than now suspected. For AT&T internalizes precisely those responsibilities that most companies externalize. As noted earlier, GM is not burdened with total responsibility for the novelty ratio in supplier firms, and it does not design, build or use new kinds of asphalt mixers, toll gates, and highway dividers. AT&T, by analogy, does all of these things.

It therefore *assumes managerial responsibility for maintaining a complex balance between three significant novelty ratios:*

that of its product line, that of its production technology, and that of the network itself.

AT&T's attempt to keep these ratios in balance helps explain why its R&D expenditures are significantly higher than that of other industries. And it helps explain why the *social, as distinct from purely economic, costs of innovation are higher in the Bell System than elsewhere.*

NOVELTY RATIOS AND MANPOWER

"People just aren't what they used to be,"[65] notes an AT&T executive in casual conversation. He is right.

Bell is beginning to feel the impact of the Super-Industrial Revolution: the crack-up of the cities into white rings and black cores; worker disaffection with routine tasks; mounting pressures for social services like health clinics and day care centers; the inability of trade unions to contain the resentments and factionalism of their members; the arrival of a new population of workers—young, Black, female, and angry.

It is, therefore, *not simply AT&T's products and technologies that are increasingly "new"—its employees are also new: new to the system; new to each other; new to their tasks.*

Just as one can measure the durability of a product or a technology, one can classify human relationships in the Bell System according to their duration. When we do this, we find that a sharply rising proportion of these relationships is under five years old, and even under a single year old.

Thus, rising novelty ratios are dramatically apparent in the data on separation rates and term of service per employee. Separation rates in the past five years have escalated to 50 percent, with 1969 showing the highest rate in 17 years. A crucial by-product of this high rate of separations is the increased number of employees new to the system. Almost one out of five Bell employees in 1969 had served less than one year. This was *twice* the ratio for 1962.[66]

According to the McKinsey study of Western Electric, the number of installers with less than two years' experience has soared from less than one percent to fully 16 percent since 1959.[67] In New York City, until five years ago, turnover rates were so low that the company did not compute annual rates for its records. By 1969 the annual rate reached 50 percent.[68]

If nothing else were known about an organization with these characteristics, it would be possible to predict significant problems of training, organizational structure and stability, interpersonal and inter-echelon communication. But, in fact, more is known: not only are the individuals new to the system, they are increasingly drawn from population groups that, until recently, were either minimally represented in the workforce, or that have undergone radical changes in outlook within the past decade.

In short, Bell managers now confront a work force whose sexual, social, racial, educational and ethical characteristics are unfamiliar. Whereas total employment in the Bell System has grown by 37.5 percent since 1963, non-white employment has shot up by 265 percent.[69] Thirty years ago, the women working for Bell were primarily single. Today two out of three are married. Across the board, 43 percent of Bell employees are now under 30, and almost a third are under 25.[70]

Here is how one senior Bell official describes some of the novel situations confronting "old-timers" in the system—situations involving unfamiliar personal problems, new styles, vocabularies and attitudes:

"Chief operators are learning what to do when a young operator 'freaks out' from an overdose of drugs. Plant foremen are recognizing what is meant when somebody says 'The Man is always on my back.' And the foreman is learning . . . not to expect a top management BSP on how to control the length of hair on some members of his male force. . . .

"A major social movement is under way as the product of central city high schools joins us and other big city service business in increasing numbers. And this influx is promising to create important changes in the authoritarian structure of business institutions. . . ."[71] This is a polite way of expressing the "I-won't-take-any-crap" attitude that is surprising and upsetting supervisory people throughout the system.

This new independence on the part of significant sectors of the workforce is linked with what are, from the company point of view, two kinds of educational liabilities. Both are connected with the issue of novelty.

The company's first educational task is to move hundreds of thousands of human beings into what is, for many of them, an entirely new *culture,* with its own tacit assumptions about time (punctuality), beauty (grooming), etc. They are surrounded by an invisible web-work of rules, unspoken conventions, and values that are not only shadowy and hard-to-understand, but novel, strange, and seemingly irrational. Attempts to prepare them through remedial reading and math courses, or courses in good grooming and company manners are not highly successful because we do not know much about cross-cultural education.

The second problem is to skill these people rapidly for specific work tasks. This type of training is far less difficult, but it becomes more costly year by year because the tasks themselves are changing, so that the educational input cost is pro-ratable over a shorter and shorter task-life-span.

In summary, the steeply climbing novelty ratios in Bell System manpower, when combined with similar tendencies in the product and technological categories, present AT&T management with a truly "new" internal environment. If, for example, we made a "time slice" and aggregated the 136,000 employees who have been in the system under a year, with the X new products introduced within the past year, the network components laid in place within the past year, and the machines, technical processes, and administrative procedures installed or initiated within the past 12 months, it becomes obvious that *we are dealing, in effect, with a wholly new organization—a massive company within the company. This company might be called Bell 1971 to differentiate it from the larger pre-existing corporation.*

This "new" Bell Company, in fact, created within a single

twelve-month period, had more employees than the *total* number employed in Westinghouse Electric Co., or in Boeing Aircraft or in DuPont, RCA, Goodyear, Union Carbide, or Procter and Gamble—each among the nation's 25 largest industrial corporations. The *increment* in employment at Bell was equal to the *total* employment of the nation's next eight largest utilities.[72]

What this dramatizes is the scope of the task Bell has set itself. It is as though AT&T were given crash orders from Washington to create, within 52 weeks, an entirely new 136,000-man subsidiary, complete with its own brand new hardware, its own products, etc. I know of no precedent for this on the scale now facing AT&T.

Of course, if "Bell 1971" were really a company or a subsidiary, it would have to have a different distribution of skills and resources. But its creation would, in one sense be easier. Difficult though it may be to create a 136,000-man company overnight, it is perhaps even more difficult to integrate a "company" this size into an existing one. The novelty is not walled off in a subsidiary, a single organizational entity, but diffused throughout the entire system. If "Bell 1971" were an isolated subsidiary, almost everyone else in the company could go about his or her business in the accustomed way. But the superimposing "Bell 1971" on the whole Bell System, integrating it into the fabric of the entire corporation, means that almost no one in the system is unaffected by the sudden infusion of novelty.

EXTERNAL NOVELTY RATIOS

If the management of novelty *within* the Bell System were all that its executives had to worry about, they would still face a difficult task. But *the concept of novelty ratios applies to Bell's external relationships as well.* AT&T maintains ties with thousands of supplier companies, competitors, independent telephone companies and customer firms around the globe. If one could systematically list these inter-organizational relationships and measure their duration, one could statistically confirm a radical rise in the organizational novelty ratio. Today the number of such relationships is increasing and the proportion of those that are new is climbing steeply. In every field, AT&T's external relations are increasingly novel and non-routine. A look at AT&T's political environment illustrates the point.

The New Industry Politics

AT&T, like all large companies, operates within a political environment, and is part of a network of politically active organizations, agencies and companies. Until the early 1960s Bell was the acknowledged spokesman for the communications industry. This did not mean that it won all its battles with the FCC or the Justice Department, or that other entities—the broadcast networks, for instance—did not also exert considerable political influence. Yet AT&T towered over the field and everyone knew it. Through Bell Labs it had access to the most advanced technology; Western set the pace in hardware production; and it was neither practical nor possible to end-run the network. Moreover, the system enjoyed for long stretches at a time an almost unparalleled public good will. Finally, AT&T had the advantage of the best forecasting in the industry. Its managers normally knew about innovations long before anyone else, including government regulators, and they had the luxury of lead time in dealing with them.

Today Bell is no longer the unchallenged spokesman for the industry. On the national level, both the FCC and the newly established Office of Telecommunications Policy in the White House have taken sharp new initiatives in defining national policy—often in opposition to Bell System interests. These powerful actors on the political stage have been joined by new entrants from the non-profit sector, like the Ford Foundation, the Carnegie Corporation, and the Sloan Foundation, all of whom are seeking to influence, if not define, national communications policy. Even more important, new combatants have entered the arena from the ranks of industry, itself. A partial list of these illustrates the jungle-like complexity of the new political terrain:

- Computer manufacturers, time-share bureaus, peripheral equipment makers and others in the computer industry;
- Aircraft manufacturers like Hughes and Lockheed with satellite capability;
- Public broadcasters, as well as the traditional commercial networks;
- Manufacturers of terminal equipment;
- CATV operators;
- Operators of specialized common carrier microwave systems;
- Manufacturers of microwave equipment; etc.

This new, kinetic landscape at the federal level is matched at lower levels as well. Bell companies face concentrated opposition from new forces active both in state public service commissions and in countless city halls. In New York, Mayor Lindsay's Commissioner for Consumer Affairs, Bess Myerson, and the City's Corporation Counsel were instrumental in causing the State Public Service Commission to grant lower rate increases than New York Tel had anticipated. The Commission also forced New York Tel to suspend certain service offerings pending overall improvement in the quality of service in the New York City area and actually ordered rebates in poor service neighborhoods. Similarly, we see the growth of local groups mobilized to protest the location of new plant sites and central offices or the movement of corporate headquarters.[73]

Basically, the political situation has converted from a relatively stable condition, in which a few major actors played more or less predictable roles, to a highly volatile one. This conversion applies even to the issues. In the past the issues seemed to repeat themselves. Surprises were rare. Chief points of contention were rate increases and the relationship of Western Electric to AT&T.

Today these issues shift into the background as new ones spring into the headlines: control of satellite communication; quality of service; CATV; pollution; aesthetic blight; racial discrimination; provision of adequate types of service for data users; etc.

Thus whether we examine the relationship between Bell and the other players, or between Bell and the issues, we see a sharp escalation of novelty ratios. This is dramatically reflected in the number of "first-time" events that have confronted Bell in recent years.

- 1962—First time AT&T lost sole control over a major communications technology vital to telephony: the COMSAT Act.[74]
- 1968—First major break in the traditional interconnection policy: Carterfone.[75]
- 1969—First FCC study of quality of service as distinct from rates.[76]
- 1970—First Presidential step toward creating communications policy center: Office of Telecommunications Policy.[77]
- 1970—First FCC investigation of AT&T employment practices.[78]
- 1971—First step toward creation of an office within FCC to serve as attorney for citizens groups wishing to influence communications policy.[79]
- 1971—First crack in "average cost" rate structure.[80]
- 1971—First large-scale consideration by the FCC of alternative network competition for the Bell System.[81]

In each of these (and dozens of other less publicized instances) Bell management had to cope with an essentially unprecedented political situation. The combination of fast-changing issues and fast-proliferating forces makes it harder for Bell management to anticipate the behavior of the principal actors. For example, the CATV companies ally themselves with the broadcasting companies on the domestic satellite issue while opposing them on programming. The number of cross-points or potential conflicts multiplies combinatorially as the number of participants increases arithmetically, requiring a much greater expenditure of energy on the part of the Bell System to maintain a favorable moving equilibrium.

This condition will intensify in the years immediately ahead. Rather than settling into a steady state, the political environment is likely to become even choppier and more volatile. In this environment, the consumer movement will play a significant role.

The New Consumerism

The consumer movement has been praised and attacked on all sides, yet businessmen still misunderstand it.

Despite outward appearances, *the New Consumerism is not a simple repetition of turn-of-the-century muckraking and populism.* Nor is it the New Deal antitrust fervor in a fresh disguise. It is a novel phenomenon, and attempts by corporations to deal with it in traditional terms are bound to fail.

The New Consumerism differs from all past cognate movements in five dimensions: issues, organization, tactics, constituencies, and pacing.

Issues. In Japan, where the Super-Industrial Revolution has only barely begun and the society is still completing its Industrial stage, the consumer movement is traditional. When angry housewives attacked Matsushita Electric, it was because they had learned that its television sets were sold for a higher price in Japan than in the U.S. The thrust of their protest was economic.

By contrast, in the United States, while the movement has definite economic consequences, its aims are frequently tied to quality rather than quantity. Reflecting the emergent Super-Industrial value system, it emphasizes the complex of goals termed "quality of life" rather than the unitary goal of economic success. The consumer movement thus has challenged the business community on auto safety, the efficacy of non-prescription drugs, conditions of life in nursing homes, pollution, military policy, hiring policies, corporate responsibility, and other issues in which the economic component is essentially secondary.

For AT&T this has been reflected in the demand by New York consumer groups that rate increases be directly tied to service improvements; in the delivery of old phone books to the local telephone office by eco-activists; in aesthetic objections to the location and architecture of telephone equipment towers; in the suit filed by a coalition of consumer groups before the California Supreme Court alleging that Pacific Tel and Tel, among other companies, denies "equal service to minorities";[82] in the new interest taken by the FCC in quality of service issues; and so forth.

In all these cases, economic issues are present. But they are overshadowed by other concerns. *If AT&T (and all other large corporations) were to chop their prices and profits in half tomorrow morning, the consumer movement would continue to mushroom.* For its objectives and roots are psychological, cultural and especially political. It is a response to the malaise of change, to the sense that large corporate and government systems are out of control, or that their energies are misdirected toward anachronistic goals.

Corporate retorts to the New Consumerism based on traditional economic arguments cut no ice—for the very good reason that the movement's goals are a saner, more civilized society, not necessarily a richer one.

Organization. The organizational style of the movement also differentiates it from historical precedents. The "movement" is given to spontaneous, hard-to-predict surges of passion and action. Its structures are loose and ad-hocratic rather than bureaucratic and permanent. Fed by media reportage, fueled by alienation from big organizations, New Consumerism rejects the formal structures of both political parties. Should it eventuate in a new party, as is not unlikely, it would be a new style party—temporary, informal, polycentric.

Tactics. Previous movements for social reform—e.g., the CIO, the NAACP—created disciplined, centralized structures, and attacked more or less rationally selected targets. The New Consumer movement has no strategy-making center. Thus it cannot easily concentrate all its energies on a single selected target. It has, however, the enormous advantage of being everywhere at once. It is capable of harassing, applying social karate, and then vanishing only to appear again a few days later in some other part of the field.

Moreover, while traditional reform movements faced an essentially hostile press, the New Consumerism knows how to generate colorful copy and has widespread sympathy in the press. Thus *Esquire* describes a device for cheating on toll calls.[83] *Ramparts* attacks not merely AT&T's involvement with the ABM, but also urges readers to "beat the system."[84] Abbie Hoffman's new book suggests that "As long as there is a phone company . . . nobody need ever pay for a call. . . . Ripping off the phone company is an act of revolutionary love, so help spread the word."[85] There follow five detailed pages telling how. More responsible groups have issued manuals to community groups telling them how to fight the phone company. Friendly newspapers publicize the handbooks and tell readers where to send for them.

Pace. Unlike mass movements of the past, whose mobilization required detailed advance planning and extremely difficult logistical arrangements, the New Consumer movement can mobilize overnight as a consequence of media exposure, can shift its resource people rapidly across the country by jet, and its ideas by long distance telephone. While traditional movements were able to focus in space (singling out a central location for action) the New Consumerism can focus in time.

For these reasons, the New Consumerism must be seen as radically different from all previous reform movements. While its present forms and heroes will no doubt fade, they will be replaced by newer, still less obviously patterned actions. For the business community this will mean a political environment that is increasingly hostile—filled with unpleasant surprises and night ambushes.

The New "Surprise" Politics

The general political situation in the United States is shifting from routine to non-routine. Starting from scratch, the consumer movement in its short five-year life span has scored numerous upset victories. All major politicians are (at least rhetorically) sympathetic to it. President Nixon creates an office of consumer affairs. Candidate after candidate attacks the corporate polluters. Magazines speculate on a Nader-for-President movement. With the rise of the women's political caucus, the possibility of a Bess Myerson political boom of some kind is not to be discounted.

Similarly, the movement has received surprisingly sympathetic support from regulatory commissions once hostile to reform. Within the past five years, public service commissions in New York, Florida, and California have ordered Bell operating companies to refund rate increases.[86] In addition, as mentioned earlier, not only is the FCC for the first time probing the quality of phone service, it is also considering creation of an office of Public Counsel to assist consumer groups in presenting their case before the Commission.

More dramatically, instances of vandalism, sabotage, and bombing are raising the uncertainty level. In this new climate, the business community can no longer continue to play by the old rules or count on its traditional allies.

Within the same few years we have seen a series of even more surprising turnabouts in the larger political arena. The Nixon economic program, imposed literally overnight, shattered the federal government's 25-year opposition to wage and price controls. Some economists believe that AT&T will be hurt by the new policies because while wages and prices in other, less easily controlled, sectors of the economy will creep upward,

AT&T's size and visibility make it comparatively easy to police. Hence, they foresee a period in which Bell prices and wages drop relative to the rest of the economy, with disastrous impact on worker morale and company profits. The fact is, however, that no one fully understands how the new policies will affect AT&T in particular and corporations in general.

Thus, according to Don R. Conlan, chief economist of Dean Witter & Co., "For all the sophistication of econometrics and models, there is no number, no person, no model that can tell what the eventual outcome . . . will be." T. D. Gibson, economist at the Security Pacific National Bank, San Francisco, complains that current economic forecasts "are probably as shaky as any made in the last several years."[87] The new political policies have made the economic outlook far more uncertain—unpredictable—than before.

Other new uncertainties in the political arena include extension of the vote to 18-year-olds. Once again, despite much complacent speculation about the "conservativism" of youth, no one can scientifically assess the impact of this new constituency on corporate behavior in the years immediately ahead. The rise of the women's rights movement and, more particularly, the women's political caucus, introduces still further volatility.

Again and again, we see a pattern in which the continuation of taken-for-granted patterns can no longer be assumed. Example: Catholicism traditionally played a conservative role in American politics. Today, Catholic liberalism and radicalism, part of a world-wide revolution in the church, make it extremely difficult to make straight-line political forecasts. Example: the rise of Black separatism offset 75 years of integrationist policy in Black organizations, tearing the Black community apart, and making Black political action doubly difficult to project.

On the international scene we witness a similar breakdown of the "old rules." The Nixon China policy, also introduced, literally overnight, shakes up hitherto predictable power relationships and increases the novelty ratio in politics. Successive currency crises and devaluations destabilize the financial system. The emergence of Japan as a giant competitor, the danger of revived Japanese militarism, suddenly force a radical revision of all our post-war Asian policies. The entry of Britain into the Common Market creates a new political line-up in Europe. West Germany's rapprochement with Eastern Europe shatters the predictable cold war line-ups and injects further unpredictability into the situation.

We see, therefore, a basic shift in the world facing Bell managers and employees. Internally, with respect to products, methods, even people and organizational structures, routine responses become less and less appropriate. Externally, in the small arena of communications industry politics, in the larger circle of corporate/consumer politics, and in the still larger framework of general domestic and international politics, we see a crack-up of old, frozen structures, and the creation of a highly novel, as yet unfamiliar environment.

THE NATURE OF NOVELTY

Novelty is another word for surprise or unpredictability, and these shifts toward higher novelty ratios—especially in the social dimension—help explain why business executives are so often taken aback by events these days. Bell managers, in private interviews, complain repeatedly about the difficulty of making necessary forecasts. This theme is dominant, for example, in discussion of the recent problems in New York.

"The curve took a sudden jump that looked like a temporary aberration," says one senior planner. "But it never came down."[88] A New York Bell officer declares: "We never in our right minds could have predicted a jump such as we had."[89] Speaking of the Wall Street district an AT&T official states: "We should have been smart enough to see it—although nobody else was. . . . The Wall Street offices had zero growth for five straight years, zero. Last year they grew 40 percent in one year in usage. We weren't the only ones caught. The market itself was caught."[90] Referring to overall construction forecasts one

AT&T planner put it bluntly: "If you had told me a year ago that we would have had this problem, I would have told you you were out of your mind."[91]

Such expressions of surprise, some taken verbatim from our interviews, are not evidence of lack of intelligence; rather, they are evidence of a significant change in the level of environmental uncertainty, which correlates positively with rising novelty ratios.

Nor is it only planners and high level executives who must deal with this new factor. The supervisor knows her operators less well and therefore cannot predict their performance as well. An engineer finds himself with a new team, and he cannot be certain of the competence of all his colleagues since they are unknown quantities to him. *Unpredictability* begins to permeate the entire structure.

It raises the stress level in the company, leads to jerky, irregular responses and, on the whole, to less competent decisions. The break-up of the old ground rules (i.e., of more or less enduring relationships between parts of the social or corporate system) means that *Bell managers, and by extension even ordinary employees, can no longer rely on pre-existing routines as safely as in the past.*

A higher percentage of the decisions made by its managers, as well as its operators, linemen, installers, business representatives and others, now require "non-programmed" thinking, evaluation and learning. More information about both the internal and external environment must be scooped up, assembled, analyzed and weighed before decisions can be made. More and more, the individual is faced with situations in which the implementation of an existing policy or procedure could lead to disaster. The individual is faced, in short, by situations in which he must *invent* a response.*

* Example: In dealing with the wage-price freeze, Bell executives and negotiators could not fall back on handy routines. They had to *invent* their responses to the new situation.

Most Bell people, however, have been encouraged to look for standardized procedures, officially approved ways of dealing with their problems. *During the Industrial Era, the company that was most effective in prescribing rules for behavior—the company with the most carefully thought out "rule book"—frequently had the most efficient organization.* Intelligent rule books codify the "most effective responses" and save employees from having to re-invent procedures each time they face a customer, a supplier, or a regulator, for that matter. *As the novelty ratio rises, however, the utility of the rule book declines, and the companies that have poured the most energy and skill into creating it are frequently the very ones least able to deal with the new reality whose essence is the break-up of the old rules.*

The positive side of novelty is that it can elicit from employees and managers alike an enhanced level of creativity or imagination in their work—provided the structure encourages, rather than suppresses, this quality. Rising novelty ratios therefore demand both a new kind of management and a new kind of structure.

We have seen how pressures toward destandardization increase organizational complexity and the problems of decision-making. The simultaneous steep increase in novelty ratios escalates the problem geometrically. As Bell moves into the Super-Industrial Era the task of leadership is somehow to manage this burgeoning complexity.

Part 4

Tomorrow's Assumptions

Chapter 6

A Model of Super-Industrialism

COMMENTARY:

In a period of intense, accelerated change, all management assumptions about the outside world have to be rechecked for accuracy with the morning newscast. But the news as spewed out by press and television presents a picture of patternless chaos. In this chapter I focussed on several fundamental changes in the corporate environment and tried to set them into a coherent frame.

In retrospect, this description of the emerging society strikes me as inadequate, not because it is necessarily wrong, but because it omits too much and doesn't adequately interrelate the factors that it does present. By 1980, when my book *The Third Wave* was published, I had expanded and deepened my working model of the new society. In that book I deal with today's profound changes in personality and community, for example, as well as the structure of elites and the "power-sphere," all of which have strong implications for communications, human relations inside the firm, and corporate organization in general. In my own work, therefore, the model presented here has been superseded by a more complex and richer model.

Nonetheless, many significant forces and movements were accurately foreshadowed in these pages. The references to the dispersal of production, for example, and to changes in the family system have been borne out. Cable television, then still a mere dot on the horizon, has expanded greatly. Japan has become a key competitor. And, if some separatist pressures have abated, as in Canada, and if New York City has not demanded its independence, it would be a mistake, in my opinion, to think that the underlying pressures for political decentralization and regional autonomy have lessened.

The continuing de-massification of production, consumption, communication, family life and other aspects of American life suggests that regions will grow increasingly disparate, rather than uniform, in the years ahead. And the very break-up of the Bell System, with the creation of seven large regional operating companies, itself reflects (and furthers) the growing importance of the regions.

Many forms of production that once required a national market can now, because of advanced technology plus the growth in affluence and population in the regions themselves, be supported on a less-than-national scale.

Similarly, while recent economic pressures have seemingly reduced the strident anti-materialism of young people, it would be an elemental error to assume that the values of the future will necessarily resemble those of the past. The mass society that gave birth to the Bell System was characterized by relatively high consensus—shared values. The America that has emerged since this report was written has moved, exactly as suggested here, toward *dissensus* and value diversity.

Moreover, the technological advances in communications now make it possible for each mini-group to have its own channels of communication, both electronic and print. This encourages social diversity and greater individuality, which then translates into a further demand for even more varied communications services.

With such fundamental transformations taking place, AT&T's managers—and a lot of other executives as well—have to rethink their operating assumptions.

REPORT:

The shift within the Bell System toward destandardization and higher novelty ratios is part of its inner transformation from a typical Industrial Era enterprise to one more adapted to the emergent Super-Industrial environment. Before we can shape an effective long-range policy for the corporation, it is necessary to begin with a model of Super-Industrialism. If America is in fact undergoing a mutation, as I believe to be the case, what will the new social structure be like?

While no one can answer such a sweeping question in detail, it may be helpful to examine a hypothetical model of the emerging society, focussing on five long-term tendencies that are already affecting the Bell System and that could have maximum impact in the years ahead.

PRODUCTION

Under Industrial society, the factory was dominant. The factory was a place at which raw materials, labor and organizational skills were concentrated. Cities became "super-factories" in which many factories were concentrated. But the factory was more than a tool of production. It fixed the mood of life, set the times when people rose and slept, demanded basic literacy and punctuality. And, above all, it served as a model for the design of other institutions, so that offices, government agencies, hospitals and especially schools began to resemble factories in their physical or organizational layout or both.

Today two things are changing this picture. We are witnessing an increasing dispersal of production out of our central urban cores, and we are on the way to the decline of the factory, itself, as the primary production tool.

As we move from a machine-intensive to an information-intensive economy, advances in telecommunications will make it possible for the human inputs to be fed into many production processes from remote, decentralized non-urban locations.

As the growth in private line communications services already indicates, the reduction of communications transmission costs will make it no longer necessary to concentrate workers in a few places and will encourage the further dispersal of work into homes, offices, lounges, specialized meeting rooms and communications rooms, where interacting groups of specialized workers meet for temporary purposes. As more and more of the important work comes to hinge on personal service and symbol manipulation, the vast Industrial concentrations are likely to break up. We may well move toward a new form of "cottage industry" based on extremely advanced technology.

This does not, of course, mean that factories will disappear, or that mass production will end. But it may well mean that the factory will cease to play a central role in our way of life, both as a productive tool and as a model for other types of institutions. For AT&T, this implies that, despite sophisticated planning efforts, Bell will need a lot of network where it does not now exist—and will have excess capacity where the network is now concentrated.

ORGANIZATION

Under Industrialism, bureaucracy was the dominant form of organization. The factory was intended to pump out standardized products; the bureaucracy was a machine for pumping out standardized decisions. Bureaucracy is based on a machine-like division of function, routine activity, permanence and a very long vertical hierarchy. Decisions are made at the top; instructions are issued; and action is taken at the bottom. This bureaucratic system is set up to perform a limited number of repetitive functions in relatively predictable environments. That is why it became the dominant mode of human organization in the Industrial Age.

In the Super-Industrial society, however, bureaucracy will increasingly be replaced by *ad-hocracy,* a frame-like holding company that coordinates the work of numerous temporary work units, each phasing in and out of existence in accordance with the rate of change in the environment surrounding the organization.

This development is already foreshadowed in many industries by the rapid proliferation of temporary organizations—task forces, problem-solving groups, project teams, and the like.

The ad-hocracies of tomorrow will require a totally different set of human characteristics. They will require men and women capable of rapid learning (in order to comprehend novel circumstances and problems) and imagination (in order to invent new solutions). In short, to cope with first-time or one-time problems, the corporate man of tomorrow will not function "by the book." Instead, he must be capable of exercising judgments and making complex value decisions rather than mechanically executing orders sent down from above.

He must be willing to navigate through a diversity of assignments and organizational settings, and learn to work with an ever-changing group of colleagues.

FAMILY STRUCTURE

Industrial societies have one standard family model—the so-called nuclear family—in which parents and children live together without the encumbrance represented by grandparents, in-laws, uncles, aunts and other relatives. This family form is by no means the only one present in Industrial societies, but it is the "ideal" form and the one most prevalent.

Several forces are now combining to overthrow the dominance of the nuclear family and to replace it with a multi-form family system. The most powerful of these forces stems from advances in reproductive technology. The social impact of the "pill" will be small in comparison with the impact of breakthroughs making it possible to implant fertilized ova in carriers, to raise embryos outside the womb, to program certain genetic characteristics, to predetermine sex of the infant, to clone humans, etc. Genetics and birth sciences are the two fields of science that seem poised for the most explosive advances in the two decades ahead.

Such developments cannot help but accelerate the crack-up of traditional family structures and the emergence of a social system based on social acceptance of many alternative family forms ranging from the familiar nuclear and extended to the communal, the aggregative, the homosexual childrearing unit, the kibbutz model, and, perhaps, "professional parenthood." All this suggests not simply changes in economic consumption and distribution but vast changes in communications needs and organizational forms in the society. It also foreshadows major changes in the needs and expectations of Bell's female employees, as is already apparent in their demands for more day care facilities and increase promotional opportunities.

NATION STATES

Two pressures are also converging to change the distribution of political power in the high technology nations and in the world. Under Industrialism, power is concentrated in nations and, more specifically, in the national capitals. Today Washington, Tokyo, London, Paris, Moscow are centers of world power.

The powerful destandardizing pressures building up in the rich countries demand a basic redistribution, with more power flowing downward to sub-national units. These pressures can be seen in their most extreme form in demands for actual secession. In Canada, for example, there is at least a possibility that Quebec will either opt out of the nation altogether, or force a basic change in the nature of the federal compact. In the United States we can expect similar pressures. We should expect demands for secession of New York City, not merely from New York State but from the U.S. itself. Demands for community control by Black neighborhoods, attempts to decentralize cities, the revenue sharing proposals of the Nixon administration, the Supreme Court decision dealing with the right of the Amish to keep their children out of public schools, all point toward a basic downward shift of the locus of power in the society. The thrust of the society is toward fragmentation rather than unity, toward devolution of power rather than further concentration.

At the same time, a set of equally powerful pressures is operating in the opposite direction. Just as power is beginning to flow downward from the nation to sub-national entities, it is also beginning to flow upward from the nation to supra-national entities. The emergence of international ecological problems—the fact, for example, that Swiss chemicals are dumped into the Rhine and affect Germany, while German chemicals are dumped in the Rhine and flow into the Netherlands—demands regulatory authority at a level above that of the nation. The move toward Europeanization reflects this tendency, as do the great number of little-known or understood international agreements having to do with the regulation of various industries (air transport, for example), weather forecasting and modification efforts, control of the seabeds, etc. The rise of the multi-national corporation, whose influence spills over national boundaries, will accelerate this upward flow of political authority.

The consequence of these seemingly paradoxical pressures will be to move considerable power out of the nation and the national capitals over the next twenty years.

VALUES

Equally important, Super-Industrialism will bring its own value system to replace the traditional value system of Industrial society.

Particularly significant for the business corporation is the coming crack-up of the structure of values built around materialist goals. The youth revolt, the hippie phenomenon, the ecology movement, the swelling interest in the occult, the reluctance of many middle class young people to accept jobs which reward them only in money, and their insistence, instead, on work that is "meaningful," "fulfilling," or "socially useful"—all these are evidence of the powerful wave beginning to carry us away from the materialist value system of Industrialism and toward what might be called "post-economic" value systems.

The post-economic value systems characteristic of Super-Industrial society will demand new standards of performance for corporations and the people they employ. So long as basically affluent conditions prevail, the concerns of individuals and society itself will shift away from economic goals toward psychological, moral, social and aesthetic ends.

Economic recession brings with it a partial regression toward more materialist values, but, barring a complete economic depression, it is unlikely that we will return to a blind acceptance of traditional economic values.

Closely linked to this decline of economic success as the primary energizing personal value is the question of economic and corporate growth. Public discussion of the Club of Rome report, *The Limits to Growth,* which stresses the conflict between resource limitations, ecological strains and population growth, reflects the loss of public confidence in the growth goal.[92] The Club of Rome model can be attacked as unsophisticated, but corporate managers would be foolish to underestimate the impact of the report. In France, in Japan, in Germany, in Holland and elsewhere, the issue of growth or no-growth has become an intensely polarizing political one, with top government officials and political leaders taking part in the debate. The fact that the report produced less of a thunderclap in the United States does not mean that the issues it raises can be ignored.

The newly emergent value system and its implicit questioning of economic growth is evidenced in statements such as that by President Nixon to the effect that "never has a nation seemed to have more and enjoyed it less."[93] This questioning will intensify.

New post-economic values are apparent also in the rising public insistence that corporations concern themselves with social, as well as economic performance, and in the beginning attempts to create quantitative measures of social performance. The consumer movement and the demand of ethnic and subcultural minorities for representation on corporate boards are also linked with the idea that corporations must no longer pursue a single (economic) purpose, but must become "multi-purposeful" organizations that fit into a social and physical ecological surround.

The biggest difference between Industrial and Super-Industrial values, however, does not lie in the shift from materialist to post-economic values; it lies in the fragmentation of values that accompanies social destandardization. Businesses will not be able to take public consensus for granted, but will be forced to operate in a milieu characterized by increasing value conflict among sub-publics.

In short, the new technology is driving us not toward an Orwellian world of robotized, standardized, monotonic societies, but toward the most highly differentiated social structures in history, each of which produces its own transient sub-systems of values within the larger framework of society. Corporations will have to accommodate themselves to small, short-lived subcultural groupings, each busily expressing, propagating and attempting to effectuate its unique value set. Overlapping, conflicting, and randomly reinforcing one another, these value sets will face corporate personnel with enormous difficulties of choice and will impose extreme pressure on the integration of both personal and corporate identity and roles.

Chapter 7

What Theodore Vail Did Not Know

COMMENTARY:

Because the changes striking us today seem so chaotic, we often lose sight of their significance. It is difficult to evaluate them without a base-line for comparison.

Take, for example, the matter of size. Smart organizers have always known that too big is as bad as too small. But the general presumption under which most executives operated was that "economies of scale" increased with growth. Do most managers still take this for granted? I suspect that since the 1970s an ever-increasing number of executives have become sensitive to the "diseconomies of scale"—the barriers to communication, the lack of maneuverability, the stifling of innovation, the impersonality, the loss of motivation that so often accompany expansion beyond a certain size.

This is only one of a number of equally profound conceptual turnabouts that mark our period in the history of management.

In these few pages I tried to crystallize the working assumptions of a new generation of managers brought up on accelerating change and the shift from a goods-producing mass society to a society based on advanced technology and extremely complex, and dense information flows. To set them into stark perspective, I contrasted them with "what Vail knew."

Some of these new assumptions must have sounded strange, indeed, to Bell's more traditional managers. Yet today, more than a decade later, most of these new ideas have become part of the implicit culture of management.

REPORT:

No one can detail the outlines of the emergent Super-Industrial society. But when these five elements of the model are fitted together, they form a consistent pattern. When we add what is known about the increasing pace of activity, the breakdown of social order underlying our legal systems, the fragmentation of religion, and the outlook for technological innovation, a still larger cohesive picture emerges on which to base certain operating assumptions.

In Part One, I pointed out that managers operate on the basis of a set of (usually implicit) assumptions about the directions of change in their society. I listed the set of basic assumptions on which the enterpreneurs of Theodore Vail's generation based their plans and strategies.[94]

When management's assumptions no longer correspond to social reality, however, it becomes impossible to set clear or realizable goals, or to implement them efficiently. Because the Industrial order is dying, today's successful managers can no longer take for granted the assumptions of the Vail period—assumptions that still seem like second nature to most of us today. As the Super-Industrial Revolution matures, managers will need a fresh set of working assumptions. And these may fly directly in the face of yesterday's wisdom.

It was impossible, of course, for Vail to foresee what America would look like in the last third of the century. There were, therefore, things that Vail did not and could not know about running a corporation today. From the hypothetical model of Super-Industrialism, it is possible to infer a set of working premises for the manager. Here, then, are *some of the things that Theodore Vail did not know*. If my model of Super-Industrialism is even partially correct, here are some of the things that tomorrow's Bell System managers *will* "know" or take for granted.

• That once basic subsistence needs have been met most men do *not* want the same things out of life, that economic rewards alone are *not* enough to motivate them.

• That there are upper limits to economies of scale, both for a corporation and for governmental organization.

• That information is as important, perhaps even more important, than land, labor, capital and raw material.

• That we are moving past factory mass production toward a new system of "handcraft" or "headcraft" production based on information and super-technology, and that the final output of this system is no longer millions of identical standardized finished units, but "customized" goods and services.

• That the best way to organize is not bureaucratically, but adhocratically, so that each organizational component is modular and disposable, each unit interacts with many other units laterally, not just hierarchically, and decisions, like goods and services, are custom-made rather than standardized.

• That the advance of technology does *not* necessarily bring "progress" and that, in fact, it may, unless carefully controlled, destroy progress already achieved.

• That work, for most people, must be varied, non-repetitive and responsible, challenging the individual's capacity for discretion, evaluation and judgment.

[See Chart next page]

COMPARISON OF INDUSTRIAL AND SUPER-INDUSTRIAL BUSINESS ASSUMPTIONS

WHAT THEODORE VAIL KNEW	WHAT THEODORE VAIL DID NOT KNOW
a. That most men want the same things out of life, and that for most of them economic success is the ultimate goal, so that the way to motivate them is through economic reward.	a. That once basic subsistence needs have been met, most men do *not* want the same things out of life, that economic rewards alone are *not* enough to motivate them.
b. That the bigger a company, the better, stronger and more profitable it would be.	b. That there are upper limits to economies of scale, both for a corporation and for governmental organization.
c. That labor, raw materials and capital, not land, are the primary factors of production.	c. That information is as important, perhaps even more important, than land, labor, capital and raw materials.
d. That the production of standardized goods and services is more efficient than one-by-one handcraft production in which each unit of output differs from the next.	d. That we are moving past factory mass production toward a new system of "handcraft" or "headcraft" production based on information and super-technology, and that the final output of this system is no longer millions of identical standardized finished units, but "customized" goods and services.

WHAT THEODORE VAIL KNEW	WHAT THEODORE VAIL DID NOT KNOW
e. That the most efficient organization is a bureaucracy in which each sub-organization has a permanent, clearly defined role in a hierarchy—in effect, an organizational machine for the production of standardized decisions.	e. That the best way to organize is not bureaucratically, but ad-hocratically, so that each organizational component is modular and disposable, each unit interacts with many other units laterally, not just hierarchically, and decisions, like goods and services, are custom-made rather than standardized.
f. That technological advance helps standardize production and brings "progress."	f. That the advance of technology does not necessarily bring "progress" and that, in fact, it may, unless carefully controlled, destroy progress already achieved.
g. That work, for most people, must be routine, repetitive and standardized.	g. That work, for most people, must be varied, non-repetitive and responsible, challenging the individual's capacity for discretion, evaluation and judgment.

Chapter 8

A Temporary Goal

COMMENTARY:

In an economy growing more complex and diversified with each passing hour, it is inevitable that many companies find themselves deep in identity crisis.

The more differentiated the environment, the more important it becomes to know what business one is in—and the more difficult.

The issue of corporate self-definition arises in every company: Are we golf ball manufacturers or are we in the recreation business? Should our airline own hotels? If we run a movie company and a sugar plantation, what exactly are the criteria that can help us decide whether or not to manufacture avionics? And as a computer-leasing firm or insurance company why do we own, of all things, a literary agency? All such problems pose questions of self-definition.

Is it important that a company have a coherent program or mission that goes beyond financial criteria? Assuming they meet profit requirements, does any combination of businesses fit together as well as any other? In short, does identity matter?

For AT&T, Universal Service was the glue that held the company together conceptually when its basic product was what old-timers called "POTS"—plain old telephone service. But in a fast-changing, more complex, continually demassifying environment, POTS was no longer enough, and it became critically important to know whether the company was essentially renting telephones or providing access to its switched network. And if so, to what kind of equipment and for what purposes? Was AT&T in the computer business? Should it be? Was the network itself a giant computer? Did this put the company, willy-nilly, into the information business? Of course, its directories made it an information collector and publisher—but should it also collect and distribute other kinds of data electronically? If Uncle Sam was going to allow others to hang their equipment on AT&T's lines, who was responsible for service quality? And if not AT&T, who then becomes responsible for Universal Service?

Without answers to these and similar questions, how could management deploy resources intelligently?

A coherent mission is a potent tool. It can help the decision-takers cut through clutter and complexity.

In practical terms, it not only tells decision-makers what to do; more to the point, it helps them know what *not* to do.

But a mission statement written when there were very few telephones in North America, and which advised the company to be all things to all people, is little help in coping with overchoice. Based on anachronistic assumptions, the old mission of Universal Service no longer provided guidance to AT&T's decision-makers. Instead of helping them to select from the expanding menu of strategic possibilities, it effectively made all options equal.

Bell's *raison d'être* was simply no longer valid. Which is what an identity crisis is all about.

That crisis is not yet over. The shift from a highly constrained, regulated company to a largely deregulated company has opened a myriad of confusing new opportunities for AT&T. Almost overnight, its managers have gone from underchoice to overchoice. And the real process of self-definition has only just begun.

Much the same is true for thousands of other companies caught up in today's whirlwind of change. Yet how many of them are ready to undergo the excruciating self-examination that Bell's mangers voluntarily carried out—years before government edict forced them to?

REPORT:

Just as the businessmen of the Industrial Era internalized a set of principles or expectations, businessmen responsible for steering large corporations through the Super-Industrial Revolution must also operate from some set of guiding expectations. It is only by creating a model of Super-Industrial society and inferring principles from it that appropriate goals can be formulated.

Lacking such a model, it has been difficult for Bell to formulate fresh goals as old goals were achieved. Thus, until the mid-50s, the simple goal of "Universal Service" was sufficient to help Bell executives make decisions. But as the variety of products, services, technological options and consumer demands all proliferated, and a condition of overchoice was created, the clear vision of the past became cloudy.

At the level of rhetoric, the old ideal prevailed. Thus, according to one senior official, at least until the 60s, "if you asked the chairman . . . or the then-president of this company what business we were in, he'd say . . . 'We're interested in serving *any* communications need that anybody's got!' "[95]

At the level of action, however, this prescription was proving increasingly useless. Faced with the need to make hard and rapid choices among technological and economic alternatives, Bell managers soon found that it was impossible for Bell to be all things to all people. What was needed was a new—and narrower—mission.

For a goal to be useful, it must be constraining. It must help AT&T managers decide what AT&T should *not* do.

A useful goal must meet other criteria as well. It must be simple and clear enough to lend itself to communication throughout the company, so that even the newest operator or installer can understand it. It must be morally energizing, providing Bell employees with a moral-building image of their own activities. It must dovetail with the larger goals of society-at-large and must help outsiders understand what Bell does and why it is important. It must concern itself with social, as well as purely economic, factors. And it must be seen, right from the start, as temporary—i.e., subject to continual review.

Starting from the model of Super-Industrialism sketched earlier, and from the managerial assumptions that flow from it, it is possible to design a new goal for the Bell System in the period ahead.

I shall argue that the purpose of the Bell System is *not* to manufacture equipment; it is *not* to run a network; it is *not* to provide a second or third pink telephone for every home; it is decidedly *not* to meet every communication need that someone in the society thinks up and is willing to pay for.

I would argue, instead, that the purpose of the Bell System in the period ahead can be spelled out as follows:

> It is the mission of the Bell System to assure the United States the most technically advanced communications system for voice and data by providing those products and services, *and only those,* that cannot be provided by other companies at equivalent levels of cost, quality, and social concern.

Instead of trying to be all things to all people, a nebulous policy that is, at the moment, damaging Bell's ability to deal even with high-priority problems, I propose the alternative principle of uniqueness to help its managers weed out activities that are of secondary importance, or that obstruct other more important activities, or that lead to corporate maladjustment in the emerging environment of the Super-Industrial society.

Careful consideration of the program to be outlined below will reveal that it is not a program for dis-integration of the Bell System, but a conscious program for the dramatic *extension of integration* over a larger sphere to be called here the Bell Communications Constellation. This "Constellation" will consist of the Bell System *per se,* along with a large number of associated companies and organizations whose activities, where relevant to the achievement of Bell's goal, will be aided, coordinated, evaluated and supervised by Bell. At every point, decentralist tendencies or devolution of power is matched by an equivalent strengthening of the center.

Only through integration over this larger sphere can the nation's mushrooming communications needs be met. To attempt to accomplish this by simply enlarging the existing Bell System through a policy of limitless expansion is a most dangerous course, threatening Bell with immobility, deadening its responsiveness, radically enlarging its employment rolls, pushing its capital requirements to the extreme, and attracting, through size alone, far more political opposition than is either healthy or inevitable.

The intention is to create a new-style Super-Industrial Bell System whose morale, driving force and social role stem from its non-fungibility. Its activities will change from year to year, its internal structure will vary, its size will fluctuate, but its stabilizing mission during the period under discussion will be to function as both the linch-pin that holds the American communications system together and the drivewheel that moves it forward as need and technological capability converge.

If we take seriously the social function of the Bell System, and regard its economic existence as instrumental to the carrying out of this function, then a series of fundamental propositions flows from this goal. For implied in it is the idea of externalizing or spinning off certain functions now performed by the System as soon as it is established that these functions could, within the expressed criteria of cost, quality and social benefit, be adequately carried out by some other corporate entity. Equally implied is the growth of certain corporate functions that are now underdeveloped, but which need much more attention. As is the case with the nation state, some power must flow *down,* and some power must flow *up,* from the center.

Moreover, since the new goal statement implies that functions will be transferred to others as they achieve the ability to perform them, it therefore also implies that *Bell's own functions will continue to change*—that Bell will always stay several steps ahead of the other participants in the communications system.

What this represents is a dynamic rather than static conception of the functions of the Bell System, and therefore a need for a more dynamic organizational form.

In short, this goal, if taken seriously, will require substantial restructuring of the System, but it will, in my judgment, lead to a much more flexible organization capable of withstanding the stresses of high-speed change that lie ahead.

Part 5

Tomorrow's Structure

Chapter 9

Organizational Problems

COMMENTARY:

To survive today's onrushing changes, we must be prepared to reconsider the very models on which our obsolete organizations are based.

The chapters that follow suggest a novel way of thinking about business activities. Instead of rigid conventional departments, the firm is divided into a highly flexible structure composed of "framework" and "modules." Instead of being treated as an isolated unit, it is pictured as occupying a position at the center (and as part of) a shifting "constellation" of related companies, organizations and agencies. The result, I believe, is a powerful model of adaptive organization.

The framework is the thin coordinative wiring that strings together a set of temporary, modular units. The constellation consists of the company and the independent or semi-autonomous outside organizations on which it relies. (This is a modification of the idea of "constellation" first put forth by the organization theorist, Bertram Gross.)

In the pages to come, this concept is concretely applied to the Bell System. The report set out to show how the world's biggest company could be stripped down and redesigned, and how the functions of its various subsidiaries might be redistributed in ways that served both the corporation and the society at large.

Before we look at the meaning of modular and framework functions, however, it pays to glance at three of the most common problems facing companies today: organizational mismatch; over-reliance on top-down hierarchy; and just plain flab—the kind that grows up when executives assume that big is necessarily better.

Every executive in a big company is familiar with these conditions. What is not so clear is what to do about them. All three were certainly present at AT&T when I first arrived on the scene. I felt they needed to be better understood before the full significance of the framework/module idea would become apparent.

REPORT:

The change in the external environment from Industrial to Super-Industrial will require basic changes in the structure of most large organizations today, including the Bell System.

The basic shift that will be required can best be symbolized by the difference between the Pyramid of Cheops and the Calder "Mobile." Classical Industrial bureaucracies are pyramidal in structure, with a small control group at the top and an array of permanent, functional departments below. The Super-Industrial corporate form is more likely to consist of a slender, semi-permanent "*framework*" from which a variety of small, temporary "modules" are suspended. These, like the parts of a Calder construction, move in response to the change. They can be spun off or rearranged as required by shifts in the outside world.

How this framework-and-module arrangement applies to Bell will become apparent below. First, it is necessary to examine three problems of organization created by the Super-Industrial Revolution.

MISMATCH

Existing organizational structures in most companies are designed to produce repetitively a few basic kinds of decision.

Under the traditional bureaucratic system, for every problem in the environment, there is a matching component of the organization—marketing, manufacturing, finance, etc. Since the types of problems are limited and repetitive, problems need only be plugged into the appropriate unit, like jacks into an old-fashioned switchboard.

Today an increasing number of problems arise that cannot be neatly matched with any one component of the organization. Instead of round jacks, we suddenly find ourselves faced with square, rectangular, and polyform jacks that simply do not mate properly with any of the existing organizational units. What is more, they come through at a faster and faster clip and it is increasingly difficult to predict the sequence in which the new problems will arise.

The result is a growing number of mismatches between the organizational structure existing at any given moment and the requirements at that moment. The wrong kinds of problems go to the wrong departments for solution, or problems are misconceived, bent out of shape to fit pre-existing organizational lines, or the departmental lines themselves are continually gerrymandered in a futile search for the "perfect" permanent organization.

This means rising structural inefficiency and continual reorganization, so that any new table of organization has a low life expectancy.

At the level of sub-units, the acceleration of change—consumer needs, social trends, political forces, demographics, etc.—means that the corporation faces an ever more rapid flow of "one-time" opportunities and problems. The faster the pace of change, the less the continuity in society and the less likely it is that tomorrow's problem will resemble today's.

A "one-time" or temporary problem, however, requires a "one-time" or temporary organization to resolve it. It is obviously inefficient to build a full, permanent structure to deal with a problem that will not be there after a fixed interval of time. The result is a necessary proliferation of modular, temporary, or self-destruct units—task forces, problem-solving teams, *ad hoc* committees, and other groups assembled for a special and temporary purpose. Some of these can be extremely large—as in NASA. Some may be designed to last many years; others, only a few days.

If it is true that the rate of change will accelerate sharply in the remaining years of this century, then we must expect a vast increase in the number of organizations and sub-organizations created for temporary purposes. This shift from permanent to ad-hocratic forms is, in fact, a vast and fundamental adaptation by society to the imperatives of high-speed social change.

HIERARCHY

Sharply vertical hierarchies, with orders flowing smoothly down a chain of command, have long been regarded as extremely efficient, and this form of control is characteristic of Industrial Era organizations.

This control system, however, is dependent upon two factors: heavy and accurate feedback from the field; and relative homogeneity in the types of decisions required. Where the kinds of problems faced by the decision-maker are repetitive and few in type, managers are able to collect a great deal of information about their problems and they accumulate usable experience from their previous errors and successes.

Today the strict vertical hierarchy is losing its efficiency, because the two fundamental conditions for its success are disappearing. Decision-makers are increasingly confronting more and more varied types of decisions, so that, along with all the complex techno-economic decisions, they are increasingly burdened with political, cultural and social responsibilities as well. At the same time, the feedback from the field is increasingly inadequate.

In absolute terms, there is more information flowing up to management than ever before in history, and far more than the individual manager can absorb and cope with. Yet, relative to the scale and diversity of the problems facing him and to the accelerated pace, the feedback is extremely poor.

The Super-Industrial Revolution radically diversifies the economic, technological and social environment within which the corporation functions, and it demands more varied and rapid responses from the corporation. Because patterns of demand, opportunities and pressures change more swiftly than ever before, there is less time for relevant information to flow up the various levels of the hierarchy or for top managers to accumulate a great deal of experience with any one kind of problem. The distance between top and bottom is not merely a question of size or number of echelons, but also of the variety of data to be processed.

In consequence, effective decisions today must be taken at lower and lower levels within the organization. Demands for participation thus do not flow from political ideology, but from a recognition that the system, as structured today, cannot respond efficiently to the fast-shifting environment. This is why we begin to see demands for political decentralization, for revenue sharing, for grass-roots involvement, local autonomy, etc.

SCALE

Many corporations, and AT&T in particular, face the possibility that further growth will prove damaging, not merely to the interests of society, but to the interests of their stockholders as well. In May 1972, referring to the nation's largest corporations, *Fortune* magazine reported:

"The 500 have traditionally enjoyed higher returns on their stockholders' equity, and higher profit margins, than smaller corporations. But their advantages on both counts have been sharply cut back during the past eight or nine years, and there was no sign during last year's recovery that the trend was being reversed. . . . It . . . seems possible that a good many of the largest companies have exceeded the size at which their operations would yield optimum profit—i.e., that size increasingly involves diseconomies of scale."[96]

It is not the purpose of this report to analyze Bell in terms of scale effects. But there is no question that the problem is a serious one. Current growth curves, if extrapolated to 1985, produce a picture of a company exploding out of control.

The challenge facing Bell in the decade ahead is how to fulfill its commitments to the public and to its stockholders without suffering from gigantiasis, hardening of the decisional arteries and ultimate breakdown. I believe the solution to this problem is intimately connected with the questions about resource mismatching and hierarchical control listed above.

Taken together, these three organizational problems mean that AT&T, over the next decade or so, will have to evolve a substantially more flexible structure modelled on the mobile rather than the pyramid. The key to this is the recognition that while the nation's basic communications system may require the services of two, three or even more millions of people in the decades ahead, it is nowhere written in letters of fire that all of them must be employees of the Bell System. It is possible to integrate the activities of a Constellation of companies and organizations without necessarily embracing all of them in a single corporation.

Part 6

Shaping a Super-Industrial Corporation

Chapter 10

Modular Functions

COMMENTARY:

"Why did they have to mess with AT&T when we already had the best telephone system in the world?"

The question is asked again and again. Many complicated answers have been offered—and mostly rejected by the public. But the real answer is simple: A telephone system, even if it is the best in the world, is simply not good enough.

Any country moving beyond the smokestack phase needs decentralized, high-speed, high-capacity networks for moving vast amounts of computer data, video images, and other kinds of messages, along with voice-to-voice telephone communications.

The United States could not run for five minutes without these additions to the telephone system. And a truly 21st century communications system could not be built by an oversized, overcentralized, overconstrained organization of the kind AT&T was before the great break-up.

This is the hidden structural reason for the transformation of AT&T, and this is also why today Britain, West Germany, France and Japan are all planning to restructure their own telephone companies. Still agonizing over the precise form of their new institutions, torn between centralizers and decentralizers, nationalizers and privatizers, all of them are studying the new AT&T with intense interest.

To have kept AT&T's old structure would have guaranteed America's loss, before long, of its claim to the world's most advanced telecommunications. As early as 1972, therefore, when I wrote this report, the question facing the country was not *whether* to break up the old system, but how.

In this chapter I began to lay out an actual strategy for the Bell break-up. In doing so, I stepped on many toes. Using the concept of framework and modules, I called for spinning off key functions of the company and attacked Bell's policy of vertical integration. I challenged both the U.S. government's demand for the divestiture of Western Electric and AT&T's theological insistence on continued ownership of its manufacturing arm. (Both, it seemed to me, missed the point.)

More important, the strategy proposed in these pages reconceptualized the role of R&D in the company, suggesting that a high-powered research unit could also be turned into an "enterprise-generator" and profit-maker. (Alas, this suggestion has not yet, to my knowledge, been implemented, even though Bell Labs' future might well hinge on it.)

Finally—and this was the hottest issue of all—I suggested that AT&T need not own its operating companies outright. This was a frighteningly unacceptable idea in 1972. Not wishing to alienate Bell management completely, I put the idea as delicately as I could. But I regarded the spin-off of the operating companies, at least in part, as an essential element in any strategic reconfiguration of the System.

What was then a set of heretical proposals for internal discussion inside AT&T has become a raging controversy in the nation—and around the world. It can be argued that by adopting (or being forced to adopt) some of these strategic policies, AT&T has exposed itself to unprecedented risks. Yet I believed then, and still do, that failure to move in the general directions suggested here would have meant even greater risks—not merely for AT&T, but for the United States as well.

REPORT:

One can imagine the Bell System of the future as the intelligence center of a large Constellation of companies and organizations all working toward the maintenance and further development of the nation's voice and data communications capability. In order for Bell to serve in this way, it need not grow larger at all. Indeed, while the Constellation itself would no doubt expand along with the country's communications needs, Bell, as the center or core of the Constellation, could grow slimmer, tighter and stronger. Its influence and its power to integrate communications would be greatly extended.

Thus, Bell must be careful to retain tight control over technical quality, research and development, major investment decisions, planning, training and coordinative activities, and other such functions to be discussed more fully below.

By combining these policies—the creation of the Constellation and outward movement of certain functions on the one hand, and the strengthening of Bell System control functions on the other—AT&T could:

- regulate its growth
- reduce its employment
- reduce direct capital burdens
- reduce decision-making load at the higher levels of the corporation
- increase flexibility in resource allocation
- greatly strengthen itself politically by creating a vast network of local and national supplier firms and Constellation associates whose interests will overlap those of the Bell System

Such changes would, in my view, enhance the corporation's ability to deal with high novelty, to experiment, to confine the impact of error or disaster, and transform itself into an organization whose essential product is leadership.

Most important, the combination of these policies will make possible a fundamental conversion of AT&T from a pyramidal organization to its Super-Industrial form based on the idea of a semi-permanent "framework" and less durable "modular" pieces. (In the remainder of this report, I shall distinguish, therefore, between "Modular Functions" and "Framework Functions.")

The creation of the Constellation should begin with the outward transfer of certain functions from Bell, itself, to other companies or organizations that will help form the Constellation. In pursuit of the proposed goal, Bell managers ought, therefore, to pay particular attention to certain candidates for transfer:

1. Activities that involve simple, repetitive, Industrial-style work.
2. Activities that are capital intensive.
3. Activities that are socially or politically controversial.
4. Activities that can be carried out more economically through piggy-backing on someone else's capability.

With these criteria in mind, let us examine the present organization.

WESTERN ELECTRIC

Historically, critics of AT&T have demanded divestiture of Western Electric on grounds that Western fattens Bell profits by padding the price of equipment. AT&T has countered by contending that Western can produce better equipment cheaper than anyone else, and that it must remain part of the Bell System because of its tight connection with the research and development process.

This debate, however important it may have been in the past, obscures certain larger, and, in my view, more important issues.

These larger questions revolve around what kind of corporation AT&T wants to be in the future.

Until now, Western executives have by and large unconsciously shaped the future of Western each time they have made a "make-or-buy" decision. These decisions have been based on considerations of economy, strategy and complexity. Thus, as the McKinsey report on Western explains, "Wisely made make-or-buy decisions . . . help fulfill the objectives of cost avoidance and cost reduction, and they help make the best use of existing plant and capital equipment."[97] Here, economic considerations are primary. Western executives have also attempted to follow the strategic guidelines set in Company Instruction 10.10 which orders them, in general, to *make* those items that "are in, or directly controlling or affecting, the communications paths" and to *buy* only those that are "not an integral part of the communications network."[98] Finally, they have taken into account the complexity of the item in question, and Western has set targets for increasing the outside purchase of relatively simple items.[99]

What these considerations overlook, however, is the nature of the labor entailed in production, and the kind of organization that results from it.

Today, Western employees are engaged in essentially three types of labor: 1) traditional *pre-Industrial* handcraft based on skills learned on the job; 2) traditional *Industrial* work of a routine or repetitive nature whether in the factory or the factory-style office; and 3) *Super-Industrial* handcraft and "headcraft" involving skills based on advanced technology, skills based on intensive pre-job training, and creative symbol manipulation such as that required in research, system design, complex computer programming, etc. Within Western itself we find past, present and future already represented.

Just as the textile and mining industries were characteristic and crucial in the first stages of the Industrial Revolution, followed by the chemical and automotive industries at a later stage, so, too, can we expect certain industries to assume a critical role during the transition to Super-Industrial society. Among these are the communications and information industries, but not those sectors of them that are simply modelled after standard Industrial enterprises.

The industries that will be characteristic of tomorrow, and which will be most critically essential to it, will be those primarily based on the third of these types of labor. Society will continue to need the products of routine Industrial manufacture. But industries based on this form of labor will fade in prestige, importance and, probably, profitability just as textile, mining and other such industries have done. As the Super-Industrial society develops, companies based on the third level of labor will form the advance guard of industry and will, in time, attract the best people, brains and financial support.

This assertion is, of course, impossible to "prove," just as it would have been impossible to prove to the textile manufacturers of New England or the mining companies of West Virginia that their industries were doomed to lose their central role in the economy. Yet it is consistent not only with history but also with the model of Super-Industrialism from which this report flows.

This suggests that make-or-buy decisions at Western ought to take into account, not merely the usual criteria of economics, strategy and complexity, but also their long-term effect on the balance of types of labor. Western's path to conversion from a heavily Industrial to a primarily Super-Industrial organization may lie in stripping away some of its simpler routine manufacturing functions, while retaining and developing its more complex and advanced activities, which, in general, turn out to be those most intimately linked to Bell Labs and the research process as well.

The difference is exemplified by the contrast between the manufacture of handsets and the creation of an electronic switching system. While it can be argued that other companies might manufacture adequate handsets at appropriate levels of cost and social performance, it is unlikely that any other company in the United States can bring to bear the resources and sophisticated skills required to design, build and install ESS units as well or as cheaply as Western can. Moreover, the process of converting the Bell network to ESS makes use of third-level labor and is directly linked to the research capabilities of Bell Labs.

Implied in the goal statement is a willingness to transfer to others the more "doable" parts of the Bell System's work, always, of course, under tight controls to assure high levels of technical, economic and social performance. At Western, the decisions should clearly be linked to the nature of the work.

BELL TELEPHONE LABORATORIES

Bell Labs represents one of the world's great intellectual resources and a key to the future of the Bell System. It also comes largely under the heading of an activity of the Bell System that *cannot* be carried out as well by any other corporation or agency.

The success of the Labs has been based on the concept of technical integration—the closest possible links between theory and practice, between R&D and manufacture. What is proposed here is not de-integration, which could be fatal, but the *extension of technical integration* throughout the Bell Communications Constellation—a system larger than that confined by the formal boundaries of AT&T.

Serious pursuit of the proposed new corporate goal would mean that AT&T would be progressively shedding functions and encouraging others to assume them and join the Constellation. This means that Bell Labs might be called upon to lend to others, on a contract basis or otherwise, some of the same kinds of support it now provides for Western Electric. Practically speaking, were Western to transfer some of its routine and repetitive functions to others, Bell Labs might have occasion to create additional branch laboratories where necessary on the premises of one or more non-Bell companies.

Bell Labs could, however, assume an additional critical function—that of "enterprise generator." Over the years, BTL inventions have formed the basis for entire industries. However, these have been seen as by-products, rather than primary products of BTL efforts. Moreover, because of the consent decree, Bell has been limited in how it might dispose of its patents and the amounts it could charge for them.[100]

One could conceive of the Labs, on the other hand, not merely as a support for the Bell System, but as an agency explicitly charged with the task of generating new technology-based industries or companies needed in the communications field. As such, it might go beyond passive licensing and actively help organize new businesses for the exploitation of its patents, perhaps on a "temporary joint venture basis" with existing outside companies. Thus BTL might help create a new corporation in a high technology field on the understanding that it would share in equity for a fixed number of years, after which it would dispose of its holding. This temporary arrangement is consonant with the ad-hocratic, modular organization, and would serve two purposes: it would reassure those who fear undue economic concentration, while at the same time guaranteeing that BTL could not rest on its honors. Over the long term, it could mean more rapid and efficient exploitation of BTL innovations and, since BTL's equity participation would exist during the early, high-growth years of various new enterprises, it could generate significant capital for the Laboratories.

Whether the "enterprise-generator" function is adopted or not, the Labs will, of course, continue to change as the frontiers of scientific and technical knowledge expand in unlikely directions. Thus one may imagine a significant growth in the life sciences, for example, or in the technology of sensing devices, or in any of a number of fields now regarded as tangential to telephone communications and data transmission. It is also likely that, if the corporation adopts the new goal proposal, the Labs would interact with other components of the Bell System at more points than is the case today when BTL's primary influence is routed through Western Electric and a liaison group at 195. Far more complex internal linkages would be required, some of which will be discussed below, under "Environment."

THE OPERATING COMPANIES

Bell operating companies today face a mounting list of difficulties including rapid growth, extremely large capital needs, high turnover rates, vandalism, physical security, handset losses and increasing political resistance. Many of these difficulties might be eased by application of the proposed new company goal.

If we firmly apply the principle that Bell will provide *only* those products and services that others cannot supply at equivalent levels of cost, quality and social concern, then it would appear that many of the functions now carried out internally by the operating companies could, in fact, be carried out by others—sometimes with great benefit for all involved.

Over the years operating companies have, at one time or another, contracted out a great variety of functions from tree-trimming and most conduit work to preparation and delivery of the directories.[101] While there have, of course, been difficulties with some of these experiments, it would be extremely healthy, for the future of the system as a whole, if ways could be found to effect the transfer of many additional functions, while guaranteeing economic and social quality control.

In inner city areas, for example, a strong case can be made for contracting out to Black, Chicano and Puerto Rican–owned companies, or neighborhood cooperatives, many of the repair, maintenance, installation and disconnect responsibilities now carried by the operating companies. Locally owned contractors, operating under close supervision, would have easier and safer access to home and business instruments in high-risk areas. In a period of increasing social diversity and rising inter-group tensions, Bell subsidiaries are likely to find their day-to-day field operations increasingly hampered by traditional policies favoring intramural work and standardized business practices. Bell Canada, on the other hand, has found that its policy of contracting a great deal of local work to small French-speaking companies has paid off in far better community relations in Quebec than would otherwise have been possible.[102]

The contracting-out relationship, however, implies the pre-existence of adequately financed, equipped and trained contractors. An alternative arrangement that has already been aired for discussion is based on the franchising model and may be more practical in fields in which ready-to-go contractors do not exist. Thus, Henry Boettinger in a discussion paper dated 7 April 1970 writes:

"One analogy would be the relationship between automobile dealers, who are 'independent' businessmen, and the automobile manufacturers who design and produce the product, arrange its financing, advertise it nationally, back up the guarantees, and train the dealers' employees in the maintenance of the line."[103]

Following this line of argument, Boettinger asks whether coin telephones could not be owned by local businessmen licensed by Bell, and responsible to Bell for their installation, upkeep, and certain collections. The local franchisee or licensee would do his or her own hiring, and, through knowledge of local economic, social and political conditions could do a sensitive job of locating and relocating phones, dealing with local police and other agencies, while having his people trained by Bell at cost.

The same principle, with modifications as necessary, could be applied to the operation of motor pools, the removal of disconnected stations, certain business office functions like collections, billings and complaints, installation and maintenance of certain specialized business communications systems, etc.

Clearly, no such policy can be implemented on a large scale until adequate preparation has been made by the operating companies to provide necessary monitoring, supervision, training, quality control, financial and other support services for organizations in the Bell Communications Constellation. The operating companies should, however, be moving to develop these capabilities in the years immediately ahead with a view to making possible long-term implementation of the new Bell System goal.

Just as this means a new relationship between the affiliated operating companies and the communities they operate in, it also suggests a review of existing links between AT&T, itself, and the affiliates.

First, there is the question of number. Recent years have seen an increase in the number of principal telephone companies as certain companies have been subdivided. As the nation moves toward greater social diversity, we may expect a further increase in the number of PTS. There is nothing sacred about the number 21. As regional and local variations or internal organizational pressures demand it, further sub-division is likely.

Second, operating companies are now based on geographical distinctions. Depending upon the nature of the changes that lie ahead, it may be necessary to integrate certain services through the creation of nation-wide operating companies that specialize in a particular kind of service—operating companies based on function, as distinct from region. It is likely that some mixture of these two principles will characterize the System in the years ahead.

Lastly, there is the question of financial control. Thus, AT&T today owns more than 90 percent of outstanding common equity in 18 of the 21 principal telephone companies. Only in the case of New England Telephone, Mountain States Telephone and Pacific Northwest Telephone does it own smaller amounts.[104] Whether this tight ownership is required is open to debate. By reducing its holdings and opening a degree of ownership to the public, significant new capital can be raised. This approach has, of course, very long-term financial implications that require study and caution.

There is, however, precedent in the history of the corporation for operating with lower ratios of control. Thus, during the early formative period of the corporation—a period of high novelty and rapid change, much like our own—Bell ordinarily owned between 30–50 percent of the stock of the affiliated operating companies, usually 35 percent. This minority position was strengthened by provisions barring the affiliates from borrowing outside funds without Bell approval. Bell was represented on each affiliate's board, had full access to operating information, and maintained other controls.[105]

The reduction of AT&T holdings in the affiliated companies has more than financial implications, however. Like the transfer of certain functions outward, it is designed to deeply integrate

Bell into the local communities in which it operates. The policy of minority participation pursued by Bell in the early days was part of a conscious attempt to build local support, and it succeeded. The program suggested here—contracting out, licensing out, and sharing in ownership—would bring with it many long-term advantages for Bell.

By building into the Constellation a network of small businesses and organizations whose political interests overlap those of the Bell System, it creates allies in regulatory proceedings. It shifts responsibility for both failures and successes closer to the local level—where most of it belongs. It encourages the growth of healthy small businesses, particularly in inner city communities where the absence of a viable middle class poses serious dangers, not merely to the Bell System, but to society at large. It cuts back on Bell's dangerously swollen capital requirements and opens a source of capital at the same time.

Most important, however, it creates a system in which a failure in one place need not drastically interfere with smooth operations elsewhere, or damage the public relations image of the Bell System as a whole. It encourages small-scale trial-and-error experimentation, and permits the successes of these experiments to be adopted where relevant without being imposed where they are irrelevant. It makes the System as a whole more sensitive to local feedback, more aware of local differences and more responsive to shifting local requirements.

Ultimately, it develops the Constellation consisting of the Bell System and congeries of associated companies, organizations, service agencies and groups. The idea of a "System" is thus extended to include more than AT&T itself.

Chapter 11

Framework Functions

COMMENTARY:

Spinning off subsidiaries and contracting out can help a company become more adaptive—but it also makes it more dependent on the performance of other firms. That's why I suggested that, as Bell cut back on its own operations and organized them into "modules," it needed to strengthen the "framework" that held them together.

I pictured a new kind of relationship between a major firm and the suppliers in its "constellation." This new model of organization lay somewhere between the hands-off relationship of buyer and seller and the hands-on relationship of franchiser and franchisee.

One framework function is planning, and here one thing is clear. While my report accurately foresaw many of the key changes that have occurred in the past decade-plus, it badly misread the direction of regulatory change. Instead of anticipating the massive push toward federal deregulation in the U.S., I pictured increasingly rationalized planning at the national level and suggested how AT&T might fit into it. This, in my opinion, was the most serious failure of foresight in the report.

Readers of *Future Shock* in 1970 already knew of my grave doubts about central planning. Since then I have grown even more critical of macroplans and have publicly urged, again and again, that market forces be allowed to work in communications and other fields. I favor even more radical deregulation, albeit with compensating legal changes to protect the consumer.

Why then did I in these pages suggest such an elaborate, if not unwieldy, planning process? To understand why, one needs to remember the conditions at the time. AT&T was still a single giant company with operations and problems in every community. It was still subject to the iron constraints of the federal consent decree. It was under sharp attack on every side. It seemed likely at the time that the degree of federal control would increase, not decrease, and I felt that if there *were* to be stronger top-down planning, it ought to be coherent and comprehensive. Above all, it should be balanced with bottom-up planning which would permit users and other relevant constituencies to participate in the process.

In arguing for the break-up of the Bell System, I believe this report encouraged a freer, looser, more decentralized, and more competitive communications system.

But to recognize the creative forces of the marketplace is not to deny the need for some policy coordination that reaches beyond the scope of any individual company.

The U.S. is the telecommunications laboratory for the whole world. But to keep that lead, it will have to combine the power of the marketplace with the foresight to anticipate long-range communications needs—plus the ability to make heavy investments that may not pay off for decades. This suggests that even in an era of deregulation, there is still a role for public participation. Communications is too important to be left entirely to the short-term pressures of competition.

Nor should the future of our communications system be determined entirely by economic considerations. Communications, above all, is a social act. It is inherently cultural, political, psychological. To regulate (or deregulate) telecommunications for narrowly economic reasons is to lose sight of its primal importance. Telecommunications is part of the glue that must hold us together in a world that is quaking with change and fragmentation.

REPORT:

The transition of the Bell System from an Industrial to a Super-Industrial structure and the creation of the Bell Communications Constellation both imply a movement of certain functions downward and outward. These cannot take place, however, unless there is a corresponding strengthening of the System's integrative machinery. The ad-hocratic units or modules of the corporation must be coordinated. Put another way, effective restructuring requires not an indiscriminate "loosening of the reins of central control" but, on the contrary, a selective, controlled movement of power upwards as well.

Certain functions can only be carried out centrally. In organizational terms, these may be referred to as "Framework Functions." They are concerned primarily with coordination, the definition and maintenance of standards, and the provision of specialized services or resources not merely to Bell affiliates, but to companies and organizations that are part of the Constellation as a whole.

At first, the Framework Organization would resemble the present 195 organization. Later, certain functions now borne by 195 would have to be radically enlarged and new functions added. (For convenience, I shall use the terms 195 and "Framework Organization" interchangeably.)

Thus, many of 195's present functions would simply continue to be located there. It is obvious, for example, that 195 has unique reasons and resources for operating Long Lines. Declining transmission costs, together with rising affluence and mobility will drastically enlarge the demands on this unit, and may well require its reorganization. But its operations, at both domestic and international levels, are so directly related to maintaining the System *as* a system, that it must continue to be operated by the Framework Organization.

The array of responsibilities now borne by 195 for operations, engineering, construction, and liaison with Western and Bell Labs would also remain. As Western and the operating companies transfer certain functions, the Framework Organization would have to provide guidance, technical assistance and other support for non-Bell organizations that become part of the Constellation. The Framework Organization would, in addition, ensure responsibility for helping the operating companies, Western and Bell Labs, carry through the difficult transitions facing them. This can be done, especially with respect to the operating companies, by assistance in advance planning, by the formulation of "model contracts" or "model relationships" with outside companies and organizations, by serving as a clearinghouse for information dealing with the transition experience, etc. There would also be significant new functions with respect to the definition and application of specifications and standards—a point so important that it will be developed more fully below.

Similarly, Bell's escalating capital requirements will increase the importance of 195's financial functions. Since pursuit of the new goal is aimed partly at shifting certain capital burdens to non-Bell companies, the financial unit might be called upon to provide technical assistance to non-Bell companies from time to time, and may have to take their needs into account in scheduling. As central banker for the System, 195 will be called upon to be even more alert and fast-moving than is now the case. As novelty ratios in the environment rise, 195 may be called upon with increasing frequency to pump funds into operating companies on short notice for temporary purposes in response to frequent and sudden shifts in communications demand and financial conditions. It may also be necessary to create a program of temporary financial support for companies or organizations, contractors or franchises, that are part of the Communications Constellation. It may be necessary to create an internal SBIC or MESBIC for certain purposes. Basically, the same principle is implied here as in the discussion of technical integration. Financial integration (or, perhaps, more accurately, orchestration) will be required, but it will have to include a system larger than Bell itself.

MONITORING QUALITY

As the System moves toward greater and greater independence for the operating units and toward more flexible forms of out-contracting, leasing and perhaps even franchising, it will be necessary to devote increased attention to maintaining service standards and System compatibility. The quality control function will require several different activities. One of these will be an elaboration of the present system for working with regulatory agencies in the development of specifications. A second will be the continual development and readjustment of specifications within the System. And the third will be a consulting and monitoring operation aimed at guaranteeing that the quality standards are enforced throughout the Constellation. This may require additional technological devices for monitoring, as well as, in effect, a technical assistance group and an inspection force. Western Electric and the operating companies may be required to place technical consultants and inspectors on the premises of contractors and other Constellation units.

The Framework Organization may require flying teams of inspectors to oversee the work of affiliates and peripheral organizations and to see to it that they hew to System specifications. These specifications, however, will extend beyond the merely technical. They will include specifications with respect to environmental pollution control as well as social performance within local communities. Information collected by the inspection force will be fed back to local independent operating companies and peripheral organizations, with deviations from standard noted. In this way, the System can begin to develop a certain arm's-length independence between the monitoring function and those charged with operating activities. This independence of the inspection agency will make it difficult for shortcomings to be concealed and developing problems ought to be headed off earlier than is now the case.

Clearly, simply informing the operating companies and peripheral organizations about their level of performance, technical and social, will in and of itself not be sufficient. What this presupposes is a set of relationships between the Framework Organization and the operating companies and peripheral organizations under which continued deviation from System standards becomes cause for central intervention. Put another way, if an operating company or a contractor fails to perform, the Framework Organization may have to have "emergency powers" to step in directly and take over for the duration of the "emergency." However, the rights of the Framework Organization to do so would be explicitly spelled out in advance and the simple existence of this power would serve as a considerable incentive for independent units and peripheral organizations to toe the mark.

The quality monitoring organization or inspection force would run continuous testing of the System from the consumer's vantage point: i.e., making calls or sending and receiving other messages in a pre-set pattern designed to provide a continuing survey of operating efficiency as it interfaces with the consumer. This activity, however, ought not be limited to technical functions, but should also involve testing the System by placing orders for new equipment, requesting installation changes, and, in effect, simulating every variety of consumer demand. This continuous monitoring function would feed information into the System earlier than would be the case if the company relied purely on consumer complaints or regulatory admonition. For this reason the quality monitoring organization becomes an essential part of the feedback system required by the corporation in order to do more effective planning.

MANPOWER

Any serious effort to convert AT&T from an Industrial to a Super-Industrial structure will also require 195 to assume an increased role in the development and deployment of human resources throughout not merely the Bell System, but the Communications Constellation as a whole. The ability of contractors, franchisees and others to perform at high levels may require direct assistance from the Framework Organization. Thus, a primary manpower function of 195 will be to anticipate future manpower needs and job configurations.

Furthermore, while executives of Vail's generation could successfully motivate workers with relatively simple and uniform economic rewards, far more complex motivations are coming into play. Once past basic subsistence levels, employees increasingly demand psychological fulfillment, growth, challenge, variety, and a sense of doing work that is morally or socially worthwhile. For this reason, work increasingly will have to be tailored to individual specifications. Bell's own experiments with job enlargement are a step in the right direction. Similarly, extremely high absenteeism might be met by what innovative German manufacturing companies today call "gleitzeit" or "sliding time" schedules that permit the worker to choose his or her own hours.*[106]

The Framework Organization can assist the operating companies and peripheral units of the Constellation by designing, monitoring and reporting on such experiments, and by actively encouraging a conversion from employee relations based essentially on economic reward to more complex motivational systems.

Challenging as these problems are likely to be, however, the

* This process of desynchronization will be characteristic of Super-Industrialism under which machines will be much more closely synchronized and people less so. Today one million workers in 2,000 West German firms operate on the "gleitzeit" principle. The work day is divided into "core" time and "flexible" time. During core time everyone is expected to be on the job. During flexible time the worker may choose to be there or not. The worker may also adjust the total number of hours he or she chooses to work each month, and accrue and carry forward time credits from one month to the next. The complexities of scheduling appear to be compensated for by improved morale and reduced absenteeism, although further research is no doubt required.

task of training and retraining may well prove to be the most difficult for the Constellation. It is here that operating companies, contractors, franchisees and other associated organizations may need maximum help from the Framework Organization.

Preparation of a worker for a useful role at Bell (or any other company) requires essentially three levels of education.

At the first level, there is simple *task training*—in which the person is introduced to the specific, step-by-step procedures demanded by the job. This is the easiest part of the educational task, and is the part for which companies have most readily assumed responsibility. Most corporate training is first level education.

At the second level, there is *formal education*—through which the person is given the rudiments of literacy and "numeracy" along with whatever specialized intellectual skills are required. Traditionally, companies have relied on schools and colleges to provide this.

At the third level, there is *cultural education*—through which the individual learns all sorts of things that he or she is required to know simply to function well in the culture. This form of education is usually taken for granted. We typically assume a worker or job applicant knows his way around the community geographically, that he knows what money is, that he holds certain common attitudes toward self, work, and family, that he knows how to tell time, and that he values punctuality. In the past, companies automatically assumed that workers or applicants were culturally prepared, simply by virtue of being members of the culture. It was further assumed that the society at large provided cultural education, rather than the school, the college, or the business enterprise.

In the decade ahead, Bell may have to take on many of the educational functions hitherto assigned to the public school system, the colleges and universities, and even some of those previously carried out by the society itself. It is naive to assume that the problem of worker preparation can be shifted back to the educators and the society, at least for many years.

The schools and colleges, themselves caught up in the turbulence of the Super-Industrial Revolution, are in deep disarray, their leaders at sea about future goals and organizational forms. It is unlikely that they will be able to sort themselves out sufficiently in the decade ahead to assure the Bell System, let alone the Constellation of which it is a part, a reliable supply of adequate manpower. The schools are having greater, not less, difficulty in teaching even the most basic rudiments of reading, writing and arithmetic. In fact, because the occupational structure differentiates and turns over at a faster rate than the educational structure, it is highly probable that the gap between the needs of the Bell System and the output of the education system will widen.

At the level of formal education, the Framework Organization may have to help the operating companies and other Constellation organizations by designing effective remediation materials to make up for the failures of the formal education system.

But this will be simple compared with the problems they will face at the level of cultural education. It is no longer possible for Bell to assume that a worker or applicant has been socialized by "the" culture, since the dominant culture is fragmenting and subdividing. The question is which *sub*-culture does he come from, and what has that sub-culture taught him in the way of cultural skills, values, language, etc. Since the process of deep destandardization occurring in the Bell System applies not only to job skills but also to life styles and *sub*cultural forms, we must expect ethnic, sexual, religious and other such differences in the Bell workforce to amplify in the years ahead. This means that problems of cross-cultural communication within both the System and Constellation will intensify.

It is here that the Framework Organization will be most needed. The public schools, colleges and universities know very little—perhaps less than the Bell System itself—about third level education. To achieve even modest effectiveness, techniques must be developed that do not yet exist, and a whole theoretical breakthrough in learning theory will be required.

Were Bell to simply wait for advances in these fields to take place in existing educational research centers, it might well find itself progressively crippled by lack of adequately skilled manpower for even the simplest jobs in the System.

Just as Bell Labs had to do pioneering work in hard technology to provide Bell with needed tools, so, too, will the Framework Organization have to develop new educational-training tools for the System. The level of work outside is too poor and the pace of progress too slow to rely on others to solve the problems in time.

For these reasons, the Framework Organization will have to concentrate considerable resources on research and experiment in learning theory, cross-cultural communication and pedagogical methodology. (Since many of the problems at this level are common to large employers, Bell might join with other corporations, and perhaps with the government itself, in organizing this effort.)

One can picture, ten years from now, an integrated learning system in the Bell Communications Constellation: a highly decentralized "University of Communications" open not only to Bell employees and those of other companies in the Constellation, but even to outsiders on a course fee basis. Such a university could make effective use of television or Picturephone, teleseminars, computer-aided instruction and other technological tools, while, at the same time, relying primarily on face-to-face instruction, game-playing, simulation exercises, and the like. It could, on a contract or fee basis, actually conduct certain classes in the high schools and vocational training schools. The Framework Organization would serve this university by supplying it with specially designed task-training aids, remedial packages, and, especially, by developing new approaches to "cultural training" and cross-cultural communication.

Finally, as change in the Constellation and in the society at large both accelerate, the personal disorientations and dislocations induced by change are likely to intensify. These result not merely in personal upset, but in lowered work performance. An extension of the "cultural education" may well have to be "coping education'' through the creation of situational groups, crisis centers, halfway houses, and other coping tools to help employees deal with stress-producing life transitions—promotions, transfers, residential relocation, retirements, births, deaths, marriages, family break-ups—where these changes influence work performance. Such services go far beyond present conceptions of ''industrial psychology'' in that they are premised not on achieving a static, productive worker, but individuals capable of coping with frequent changes on and off the job. Here, too, new territory must be covered. No one knows how to do these things well, and Bell, in order to protect its own interests, may well have to do pioneering work that will, in the end, turn out to be of value to others as well.

ENVIRONMENT

AT&T (like all corporations) depends on the reliable functioning of a network of social institutions ranging from police and sanitation services, to churches, community centers and schools. As these malfunction, because of the upheaval associated with the Super-Industrial Revolution, it may be necessary for the corporation either to take on some of their functions, or to provide selective support to them so that they themselves can carry out their functions.

This is not to suggest that any company can, or ought to, attempt to replace government services or to return to the paternalist policies of the past. What it does mean is that Bell can no longer take for granted the implicit support it has received until now. The schools provide a clear example. As noted above, if Bell wants an adequate supply of manpower, it will have to provide certain forms of remedial education to make up for the failures of the schools. Simultaneously, Bell operating companies and other components of the Constellation may have to provide back-up to local schools to help them with their problems.

The provision of day care centers, certain transportation problems, security problems for female employees, etc., can all be traced to the failure of public services, and in each of these areas Bell is already considering means of compensating for the public failures.

This pattern will become more pronounced, and an important Framework function will be to help Constellation companies and organizations devise compensatory programs and/or support programs for their local institutions, along with guidelines for their use. Under what circumstances is support for local public institutions warranted? What forms must it take? What kinds of compensatory programs can or ought the System provide? Such issues will intensify in the years ahead, as companies struggle to maintain an environment in which they can function.

Simultaneously, Bell will be required to keep track of its own environmental impacts. Any corporation as large as AT&T, not to mention a constellation of companies and organizations, produces reverberatory waves that impact on the surrounding society. In the decade ahead it is highly likely that large organizations, private and governmental, will be held more sharply accountable for the consequences of their behavior.

Broadly speaking, these consequences flow in two streams—consequences of economic and socio-cultural actions taken by the company, and consequences of technological actions. Accountability will apply to both, and will extend to secondary and tertiary consequences largely overlooked today.

AT&T for many decades has prided itself on its efforts to be a good "corporate citizen." However, the conception of good citizenship is today being extended far beyond its traditional meaning, as government and ordinary citizens become aware of the systemic nature of the social order and the physical environment. For AT&T to be regarded as a "good citizen," it will have to take concrete steps manifesting a broadened view of its own responsibility.

It must expect its *economic* actions—to build or not to build, to relocate, to hire or fire large numbers of employees, etc.—to be subjected to public scrutiny and controversy. Its *socio-cul-*

tural actions will also be intensively studied: Does it discriminate? Does it apply preferential quotas to Blacks, Chicanos, Jews, or women? Do minority employees enjoy the same chances for promotion to the very top? Does the "deposit" policy of the operating company affect different neighborhoods or groups unevenly? Does the corporation have a policy with respect to the employment of homosexuals? Do single men or women find it harder to achieve promotion? Will the company employ draft evaders? Does it impose unacceptable standards of dress or hair style? How does it preserve privacy? Does it cooperate with official wiretapping too readily? Such questions are being raised today, but one can anticipate many others tomorrow.

As rapid changes occur in the society, different criteria will be applied. An important Framework function must be the early detection of changes in the criteria of corporate citizenship and the creation of internal systems for monitoring the behavior of the company with respect to these criteria. We shall see, in the next section dealing with regulation, why the ability of the System to monitor its socio-cultural impacts may prove increasingly crucial in justifying its rate requests.

Another field in which corporate accountability will almost certainly increase is that of technological impact. It is apparent that the next decade will witness increasing public pressure for the regulation of new technology to prevent avoidable deterioration of the physical environment. These demands will inevitably move beyond questions of physical environment to include the effect of new technologies on socio-cultural "quality of life."

Certainly, within the next decade the federal government will establish new agencies for technology assessment. Its actions may well be matched at local and state levels as well. The exact nature of such agencies, the care with which they are designed, and the power they wield, will be inversely proportional to the initiatives taken by private industry.

Just as Theodore Vail, in the early history of the company, recognized the appropriateness of federal regulation of communications, it is important that the Bell System go on record early as favoring the monitoring and advance appraisal of technological innovation in the society, and that it lend its unique resources to the development of effective assessment methods.

Some scientists and engineers have grave reservations about technology assessment. They argue that advance assessment of technical innovations could constrain technological advance. Others assert that a piece of technology cannot be assessed until it is actually in place and on-line. Still others contend that systematic assessment is simply impossible under any circumstances.

These are honest contentions—but they miss the point. Technology is assessed today. It always has been. What is wrong is the inadequacy of the procedures and simplicity of the criteria. There is no such thing as "pure" or "constraintless" technological advance. Every society, through its economic and political institutions, determines which technical innovations ought to be funded, developed and diffused, and which suppressed or ignored. What is necessary now is a radical improvement of this process.

Moreover, while it is not possible to detect, in advance, all the consequences of an SST or a nuclear breeder reactor, the argument that the innovation must first be used before it can be assessed is misleading. It suggests that we can learn nothing from simulation, from modeling, from analogous cases, and from other assessment procedures. Clearly, it cannot be taken literally, since it implies that we must actually drop hydrogen bombs before we need to worry about them.

There is no question about the third objection: systematic assessment is extremely difficult, and physical scientists, accustomed to exactness and experimentation, may be dubious about the theoretical possibility of performing high-precision assessment, especially with respect to "quality of life" criteria. Indeed, the behavioral sciences, which must be involved in any rounded assessment procedure, may never approximate the physical sciences in exactness.

Nevertheless, the potential consequences of some technologies are so enormous, both positive and negative, that we can no longer formulate sound national or even local technology policy without radically better assessment methods. To oppose their development is a form of intellectual "know-nothingism" that undercuts the most basic tenets of science itself.

Furthermore, we must now seriously prepare for the possibility of certain technologically-induced disasters—a runaway breeder reactor, a trace of biological contaminant from outer space, a murderous bout of pollution—so severe as to arouse massive and violent public antagonism toward science and to corporations associated with advanced technology.

Unless the technological community and the business community adopt a responsible attitude toward technical innovation, we could face a far more serious Luddite counter-movement than that already present today. The very greatness of the contributions made by the Bell Labs to scientific and technological know-how could, under certain circumstances, prove to be extremely damaging to Bell's public reputation.

As a primary creator of new technologies, Bell has a moral obligation to the public—and an economic obligation to its shareholders—to move, in advance of public criticism, to a position of support for what might be termed "responsible technology." This means that the corporation should actively support the movement for technological assessment.

If it is true that various public agencies are likely to arise in the years ahead with technological assessment functions, some, no doubt, with the power to say no to certain new technologies, it would be wise for Bell to anticipate these developments. By participating in the move to improve procedures and to create new institutions, Bell could earn the right to help in their design.

It is difficult to overstate the importance of this issue. In my view, it will increasingly enter into the political arena—the SST defeat being only the first skirmish in a war over the future of technological development. Technology will become one of the key political issues. The Luddite notion that all technology is evil is naive and dangerous. But so is the idea that all technological advance is progress. What is needed is powerful support for *responsible technology, responsibly developed.* Bell's future reputation, not to mention its economic success, will heavily hinge on this issue. For these reasons, the Framework Organization must commit itself to monitoring, with the best tools available, the impact of AT&T's own existing technology, and to anticipating, as best it can, the effects of alternative communications technologies of the future.

With full knowledge of the difficulties and the limitations of present procedures, Bell should begin now to make systematic studies of the potential physical and social consequences of such innovations as Picturephone, cable communications, the laser—even electronic switching. It should be prepared to make its studies public, including its own reservations about the procedures used. By beginning this process now, instead of waiting until it is forced to undertake it, Bell would gain significant credibility.

REGULATION

Another Framework function likely to undergo drastic change and to assume greater importance has to do with regulation. Bell's successful transition to a Super-Industrial structure cannot easily occur without understanding and some degree of cooperation on the part of the regulatory agencies. In turn, these agencies, too, face a decade of transition.

The three most significant changes likely to affect regulation are: 1) development of a national communications policy; 2) development of wholly new, non-economic criteria for evaluating service and establishing rates; and 3) creation of additional regulatory agencies below the state level.

Each of these implies changes in the Framework Organization.

Until now Bell has operated essentially in the absence of any well-defined and comprehensive national communications policy. Policy has had to be inferred from an unrelated series of Presidential announcements, congressional speeches, court rulings and FCC and state regulatory commission edicts. As one

AT&T official recently put it: "I don't know of any one place where there is a conceptual picture."[107]

It is likely that in the years immediately ahead, a process of rationalization will take place at the national level, with attempts made to formulate a wide-ranging policy. Bell, because of its influence, history and centrality, is in a special position to help shape the new conceptualization. In addition, as Bell extends its roots more deeply into community life through mechanisms like contracting out or franchising, it will be in a strong position to act as a spokesman for systemic diversity—for responsibilities to local and specialized interests.

Bell, in fact, could well take the initiative in recommending formation of a National Communications Policy Council which might include not only representatives of the FCC, the OTP, etc., but also of cognate agencies such as the Post Office, the Department of Transportation, and, at a different level, representatives of community groups, urban, suburban and rural municipalities, consumer protection agencies, and the like.

Such a body might begin to consider communications policy in broader and more fundamental terms than is customary, taking into account issues such as the relationship of communications facilities to rural-urban balance, to regional industrial development, to social and educational problems, etc. These communications questions, which are already discussed explicitly and publicly in such countries as Japan and Canada, are likely to surface in the United States in the years immediately ahead, and will begin to influence national policy. Similarly, questions involving potential trade-offs between investment in transportation versus investment in communications, or between a more automated postal system or the more rapid diffusion of Picturephone, are all likely to break the political surface. Issues surrounding the future uses of cable television will grow even more heated than they are today. The creation of such a national agency could help define the questions more clearly, if not actually determine policy. In particular, it should be the function of such an agency to suggest new criteria for measuring the effectiveness of the national communications system.

In any case, whether or not such an agency comes into being, the FCC is likely to be transformed, over time, from a policy-making to a policy-implementing body. (More accurately, from a body that, in effect, makes policy because of a policy vacuum, to one that will make policy within broad outlines established above.) The incentives and disincentives deployed by the FCC will reflect a wider range of concerns than are currently taken into account.

Thus today the level of allowable profit is determined, in theory at least, by the rate base, an economic concept involving operating expenses, taxes, depreciation and the estimated value of plant and equipment.[108] There is rising dissatisfaction with these criteria among regulatory officials and, according to one senior AT&T executive, "There could very well be some real significant breakthroughs in regulatory thinking. . . . The regulatory process today is archaic. . . . There is a change in the direction of regulation on the basis of *production,* what you produce in the way of quality, in relation to the rapidity with which you introduce to your customers new technological equipment, with relation to the degree to which you innovate in your management functions, to reduce expenses, etc. . . . This is coming from the regulated and it's coming from the regulators."[109]

But there is something else coming, too: a new awareness of the importance of non-economic criteria. Thus, John D. Rockefeller III has contended that "improved social accounting is needed if the corporation itself, as well as the public, is to be in a position to appraise the corporation's contributions. . . ."[110] Gabriel Hauge, chairman of Manufacturers Hanover Trust, has echoed the theme, arguing that business must "broaden its system of accounting to include the full social and economic costs of production and growth."[111] These statements, among countless others by leaders in the business community, reflect a shift in basic expectations about the functions of the large corporation. They are reflected in a number of practical efforts to design new "indicators" of corporate social responsibility. It is likely that these efforts will continue in the years ahead and that they will, in time, have an impact on the regulatory process, so that social, ecological and other factors come into play in the promulgation of regulations.

It is conceivable that the FCC would, under certain circumstances, be encouraged to permit AT&T a higher rate of return in compensation for high "social performance." It is probable that regulators, under pressure from outside interests, will begin to demand quantitative data about the Bell System's investments in pollution control, its charitable contributions, support of minority entrepreneurship, treatment of consumer complaints, employment and promotion policies with respect to women, etc. It has already begun probing the issue of minority employment.

Similar changes can be expected at the level of state regulatory agencies, along with a proliferation of regulatory agencies or consumer protection agencies at the local level as well, each of them demanding evidence that Bell is a high performer on "social" as distinct from purely economic indices. The Framework Organization must assume responsibility for training a whole new generation of local, state and federal-level employees who understand the broader technological and social criteria and the ways in which communications policy comes to be formulated.

These tendencies must be seen as part of the much larger phenomenon I have termed the Super-Industrial Revolution. They are not accidental or idiosyncratic, but deep-going responses to the dislocations of high-speed change and economic growth. Any corporation making the transition from Industrial to Super-Industrial structure must take them into account, and within Bell this will mean new attitudes, and new problems for those carrying out the regulatory function.

PLANNING

The smoothness of Bell's transition from an Industrial to a Super-Industrial form will depend in large measure on the ability of its planners. Implementing changes on the scale proposed in this report obviously implies the need for a major investment in planning. Such changes ought not be attempted without careful advance assessment of alternatives and of potential consequences. But even if Bell made no change in its mission, simply to hold its own in a period of high uncertainty it would have to radically expand its planning activities.

Planners have always worked against heavy odds. Today, however, with accelerating rates of change and higher novelty ratios, the odds are clearly worsening. Bell has extremely able planners and a strong Management Science Division that could form the nucleus of the Framework Organization's planning agency. Throughout the System, Bell planners are at least the equal of their colleagues in most other large companies and government agencies, and they go to great lengths to develop data about future needs and capabilities. They scrutinize local forecasts of population growth or decline, personal income data, commercial and/or residential building plans, employment and business spending, governmental spending programs, seasonal variation in telephone usage and other factors. The problem is that, like their colleagues in other enterprises, they can no longer trust their tools.

To strengthen the planning effort, it will be necessary to link it more closely to the goal-setting machinery and to move beyond the normal technocratic assumptions and methods. The planning staff at the Framework level must serve as a change agent in the Constellation as a whole, preparing and educating planners in the operating companies and associated organizations. In the meantime, the planning function must itself be transformed.

Development of a Totally Integrated Planning System

Today no matter how capable Bell System planners may be, they operate in a vacuum created by the absence of a coherent national policy for communications and by the absence of adequate feedback from the periphery of the System—from the consumer, the community, the public at large. Both these gaps must be filled.

National Policy. Improvement of the planning effort must begin with support for improvement in national policy formulation. In the previous section on "Regulation," I proposed formation of a National Communications Policy Council to shape comprehensive national policy, thus making it possible for the FCC, AT&T, and other actors in the communications marketplace, to position themselves with respect to socially approved criteria.

The exact form that this policy-making body might take, the appropriate membership, the kinds of incentives and disincentives at its disposal, its relationship to the White House and the federal agencies—all these must be carefully thought through. Any attempt to create such a structure hastily might create far worse conditions than now exist. But such questions aside, communications services now demand so large a percentage of our capital resources, and have so profound an impact on the society, that we can no longer afford to leave policy to accident or to formulation by omission.

For these reasons, I believe it highly likely that national policy machinery *will* develop in the communications field within the next ten years, and that Bell ought to encourage this development and begin now to prepare for it. Such a Council could provide Bell planners with coherent data about national needs and goals, seen in relationship to the national communications system.

Participatory Planning. It will be necessary to complement this national machinery with new policy planning agencies working, in effect, from the bottom up. Just as it is necessary to formulate Bell plans in terms of large national goals for communications, so, too, the development of plans by components of the Bell System and the surrounding Constellation must increasingly take into account local goals.

While it is clearly not possible for Bell to undertake the repair of the whole nation's inadequate goal-setting equipment, and it cannot take upon itself the organization of generalized local goal-setting agencies, it can, and should, assume responsibility for doing precisely that in the limited area of communications.

Bell now has within its grasp an important opportunity. It can create for itself and for the nation a model of Super-Industrial planning—a system designed to provide exquisitely sensitive data about future communications needs, opportunities and dangers. It can, in the process, enlist massive community support for its goals.

Thus AT&T at present is receiving inadequate information from its periphery. The amount of feedback streaming into the Bell System is enormous—but it is insufficiently sensitive to local and subcultural concerns of a non-economic nature; it is not adequately anticipatory; and it is not focussed in terms of local or sectoral goals. Moreover, Bell people face an increasingly turbulent social environment that will make it harder, not easier, to anticipate change and prepare for it.

A key factor in determining the capacity of the System to plan effectively will be the role of the public. The public, at all levels and in all fields, is increasingly asserting the right to participate in goal-setting. The future shape of AT&T cannot, and will not, be hammered out solely between AT&T and the government in the courts or before the FCC and the public utility agencies. Increasingly vocal forces, including user groups, religious, ethnic, sexual, age, political, and perhaps even overseas groups, will begin to demand more of a say in the definition of community goals—including those goals relating to communications.

If Bell regards this development as wholly negative, resists it and becomes identified with die-hard corporate resistance, it will suffer severe political backlash, some of which may spill out of the normal political channels into increased vandalism, even escalating sabotage. Among other things, Bell (like other large organizations) can expect to face mounting resistance in its efforts to obtain data for planning purposes from consumers and other groups—unless it is prepared to "pay" for that information.

Market researchers and social scientists going into Black neighborhoods today are frequently unable to trust the replies they get to survey questions. Sophisticated Blacks often "jive" the interviewers on the principle that the information given out will either be used against them, or, at best, will be used without reference to their needs and interests. Similarly, when the American Council on Education undertook a massive survey of student unrest, activists launched a national campaign, involving speeches, leaflets and magazine articles, calling upon students to refuse to answer queries or, once again, to lie on grounds that the results would be used against student interests.

We must expect such resistance to increase. In my view, corporations will increasingly have to offer a *quid pro quo* for information. They will have to make advance commitments about the ways in which needed data will be used—that is, they will be compelled to pay in terms of *shared power*. As consumer groups, ethnic organizations, and other community forces gain adherents, they will begin to apply "info-politics" to put pressure on corporations. Lacking active cooperation, and facing the real possibility of "informational sabotage," local level planning will become increasingly difficult.

Yet the public and the corporation need each other. And there is a wholly different way to assess the present pressures for public participation. Rather than regarding them merely as an assault on management privilege, they can be seen in positive terms as holding within them the potential for a wholly new and more effective planning system with especially valuable possibilities for the Bell System because of its national and highly local character.

Thus, rather than opposing demands for participation, I believe that Bell should take the initiative in moving toward a form of "participatory planning" under which inputs from community and consumer groups are actively elicited by Bell System planners on an on-going, day-by-day basis.

In each telephone district steps should be taken to organize a Communications Council in which municipal officials, leaders of community organizations, representatives of various telephone user groups, and others are publicly invited to help design the local communications systems of the future in terms of local goals.

Such a network of groups, some geographically based, others based on functional or subcultural characteristics, would not necessarily be tidy or easy to work with. Its existence submits local Bell planning to public scrutiny and open debate, and, in effect, subjects the corporation to certain constraints.

I believe, however, that the failure to develop such public inputs into local planning will result in far greater constraints and dangers to the communications system. Conversely, I believe that the creation of such units, with Bell's active encouragement, would not only bring Bell important public relations and political advantages, but, more important over the long run, provide Bell planners with an early warning system sensitively attuned to shifts in communications demand patterns. It would also educate large numbers of community leaders about the real economic costs of telephone service and the problems involved in operating a national communications system.

The creation of local level participatory planning groups is consonant with the historic movement for government decentralization, grass roots participation, revenue sharing and community control. This movement is likely to be one of the major forces in American life in the decade ahead. The creation of community communications planning groups provides a way of meshing the Bell System even more firmly into the communities in which it operates.

Seen from the long view, it represents for the Bell System not an invasion of prerogative, but the opportunity to create a unique and powerful aid to planning. Thus it serves as the natural counterpart of the proposal for a National Communications Policy Council and it completes the structure needed for a fully integrated planning system through information which would reach the Bell System Framework Organization from both above and below.

Clearly, it would be a mistake to attempt to create the participatory planning network on a national basis all at once, or even to commit the Bell System to such a network before adequate experiment on a local and limited basis. The role of the Framework Organization, however, should be to design and carry out the life-tests necessary to make such a network possible.

(For further development of the concept of participatory planning, see Appendix A.)

More Emphasis on Socio-Cultural Variables

The creation of a totally integrated planning system must be matched by a wider conception of the kind of information that is relevant to planning. By socio-cultural variables, I mean variables reflecting political change, education, racial and religious differences, mobility, temporal characteristics, sexual and familial attitudes, and other underemphasized factors. Such factors are growing in importance, yet planners throughout government and industry have traditionally focussed so sharply on economic and demographic variables that we lack adequate data and models for introducing the necessary socio-cultural variables into the planning effort.

Consumerism, the spread of anti-war sentiment, changes in welfare, the level and types of crime, geographical and occupational mobility and similar factors now bear more heavily than ever on communications demand. So, too, do developments in transportation and other fields. It may be, for example, that the number of airline flights into or out of some community offers a better indicator of future telephone usage than the usual data on population and family income. It may be that certain communities can be classified as "information-originators" and others as "information-consumers" and that such patterns have a heavy impact on consumer demand. In turn, these distinctions may turn out to be sensitively connected with levels of education, ethnic differences, or even such variables as museum attendance.

The linkage between social change and communications use grows more intimate all the time, so that, for example, increasing drug abuse can be related to rising telephone usage. Thus, if drug abuse increases crime, it may result in more people staying home more of the time, shopping by telephone, installing telephones where none existed (in order to maintain contact with police or nearby friends and relatives, etc.). As crime rates rise, people tend to take the telephone off the receiver when they are away, to suggest to potential burglars that someone is, in fact, home. The telephone is thus converted into a crime-deterrent device. *Unless planners begin to develop adequate data on such factors, along with hypothetical models illustrating their relationships to communications, it will be increasingly difficult to make usable plans.*

The Framework Organization can play a special role in encouraging the infusion of socio-cultural data and models into Constellation-wide planning efforts, designing and experimenting with a variety of indicator systems that integrate economic, social and cultural variables.

The development of these inputs to the planning process, however, will depend upon more than academic research; it will depend upon actual involvement by Bell planners in community problems. Thus the proposal for participatory planning through the creation of Communications Councils at the grass roots level will, as a secondary consequence, vastly increase the sophistication of Bell planners with respect to cultural and social forces that are likely, in the years ahead, to have the greatest impact on the communications system.

New Planning Tools

Throughout the Constellation, planners will need new, not-yet-existent tools. The more diverse American society becomes, the more difficult the task of making sub-aggregate forecasts. The escalating diversity of Bell personnel, products and services must be tracked, inventoried, and brought together in increasingly short-lived configurations. This vast increase in the number of possible products or service configurations decreases the probability that planning for any single product, service or component will be on target.

In consequence, even economic projections for each telephone district are likely to be further and further off the mark. Rising novelty ratios also create planning difficulties. Increased novelty in the environment implies higher levels of unpredictability and volatility in both the internal and external environment of the company. Planners face an increasing number of first-time, bizarre, unusual or non-routine events. This instability—this changing of direction again and again—produces new or unprecedented circumstances and undermines the power of extrapolation as a planning method. Linear methods work best in periods of relative stability; they break down in periods of upheaval such as the one we are entering today. This suggests the need for the development of better non-linear planning methods.

Simultaneously, the acceleration of demand for Bell services means that many planning studies become obsolete before they are published. It also means quickened decision-making, which, in turn, places increased pressure on planning staffs for faster and more frequent assessment of alternatives. The most important effect of this speed-up is to demand longer time horizons of the planning staffs. The more rapid the pace of change, the longer the time-sweep required and, also, once again, the more difficult the process becomes.

In turn, this extension of the time horizon, like the decline in the power of linear methods, forces a reliance on less precise, more intuitive data and models, and produces a shift in the balance of quantitative to qualitative planning data.

Most management (and most planners) are not comfortable with this shift, having been trained to place maximum reliance on quantified data and minimal reliance on all other forms of information. This is not to suggest that quantitative data is bad or that qualitative data is better. When data can be quantified without substantial loss, it obviously should be. But planners can less and less afford to ignore qualitative data, and it is going to be increasingly difficult to package all the needed information in quantitative forms.

Across the board then, we can summarize the necessary steps for improved planning. Such steps must include: creation of fully integrated planning machinery from the supra-corporate to the sub-corporate level; the addition of socio-cultural information and models to the present economic data base; and the development of new methods involving a shift from aggregate toward more sub-aggregate planning, from linear toward more non-linear projection, and from quantitative toward more qualitative materials.

BEHAVIORAL RESEARCH

Even a quick glance at the Framework functions as defined above reveals that many of them cannot be effectively carried out today because of a single, central lack. They depend on social or behavioral data and models now lacking in our society as a whole. For example, our models of learning behavior are naive. Our understanding of the ways in which technology impacts on society is poverty-stricken. Our ability to anticipate social, political and economic turns is weak. These weaknesses are not Bell's alone. They apply as well to all companies and to government agencies. But the ability of the Bell System to navigate the racing waters of change in the decade or so ahead will demand sharp improvements in our socio-behavioral know-how.

In the Industrial Era, Bell did not wait for others to invent the technological tools it needed to meet its goals. By the same token, in the years ahead, Bell would be ill-advised to wait for others to develop the socio-behavioral tools it will need to transform itself into a Super-Industrial corporation.

The time has come to take seriously a proposal that has been made many times before in the Bell System. Today the circumstances make it urgent for Bell to create a counterpart to the Bell Laboratories—the Bell Behavioral Laboratories.

A key premise of this report is that the conversion of the Bell System from Industrial to Super-Industrial form depends on the company's ability to anticipate and respond to social and cultural, as well as economic and technological, dislocations. To meet this objective, Bell managers—and especially those with Framework responsibilities—will require strong support from a social research facility.

Such a facility could be of paramount importance in serving the operating companies and other units of the System, as well as the Framework Organization, particularly in fields like planning, environment, manpower and regulation.

One activity closely connected with adequate planning, for example, is the advance estimation of demand. Demand for telephone service is influenced by many considerations—some of them only poorly understood and mapped by social science today. Among these factors are differentiation; mobility; the pace of decision-making; the pace of social interaction; intergenerational relationships; family structure and its distribution; mass media output, etc. These factors operate in addition to the more familiar variables of population growth; increase in computer telecommunications needs; level of economic activity, etc.

The present state of social science research is such that it is possible to develop indices of differentiation, measures of social pacing, better mobility statistics, and so forth. While there is no apparent theoretical reason why such measures cannot be constructed, I know of no one engaged in designing them. The Bell Behavioral Laboratories, by constructing such measures, could not only enormously improve its own anticipatory analysis of demand, but achieve significant breakthroughs that would be of broad social utility—not unlike the impact of BTL technical inventions in the Industrial Era. It need hardly be pointed out that small increases in the accuracy of demand planning would lead to extremely significant savings through more efficient investment and deployment of manpower. A relatively modest investment in social science research could yield large economic returns.

Similarly, planners could be greatly aided in their extremely difficult tasks by the creation of a systematic network of social and environmental indicators to integrate with existing economic indicators. No system of indicators can eliminate the necessity for interpretation and judgment by managers responding to or anticipating change. But their absence compels the corporation to fly by the seat of the pants in crucial and potentially dangerous areas. The design of a system of indicators relevant to the needs of the Bell Communications Constellation is a task for the Bell Behavioral Laboratories.

The Bell Behavioral Labs would likewise enrich the work of the planners by developing broad-scale models of future social and political change, and inferring from these arrays of contingencies to be planned for.

In the field of manpower, too, such a facility could prove pivotally useful. Manpower recruiting and retention efforts will depend upon Bell's understanding of the fast-changing values of the workforce and its various segments, on such factors as differences in transience levels and temporal sophistication among employees, on the ability to do "cultural training" and to offer "coping education." All these require insights into the learning process that, by and large, are not ready-to-hand for use by Bell manpower managers. Clearly, once again, small increases in understanding, even if they yielded but small improvements in turnover rates, could pay for themselves many times over.

With respect to regulation, BBL could likewise serve an extremely valuable purpose. As regulators gradually widen the concept of the rate base to include social as well as economic factors, traditional arguments used before the FCC, the state agencies and the courts will lose much of their force. Regulatory executives will require new kinds of data, new models and a new vocabulary in presenting their case to the regulators. At present, for example, two social (as distinct from primarily economic) factors are contributing to the escalation of Bell's cost of doing business. The accelerating mobility and micro-mobility of the population and the transience of property relationships both increase Bell's operating expenses and capital needs. Yet without being able to measure and anticipate such phenomena, it will be difficult for Bell spokesmen to prepare compelling arguments that link these social trends with the hard fact of rising costs.

Similarly, the BBL, by carefully observing social trends could anticipate crises that now arrive without warning. It could create social and political models that provide an array of possible futures that help anticipate shifts in regulatory criteria, moods, and agency structure.

Such a facility, while focussing on the critical problems faced by the Framework Organization, could serve all the units of the Bell System, and the Constellation, on essentially a contract basis. Bringing together a carefully selected interdisciplinary team of researchers in sociology, economics, psychology, anthropology and communications theory, along with mathematicians, modellers, and futurists, the Bell Behavioral Laboratories would, like Bell Labs, focus on certain "enduring themes." While for the Bell Labs these themes are switching, the network, etc., for the Behavioral Labs they would include: consumer demand, economics, indicators, training, and the like.

In each field, the BBL would operate at three levels: the development of theory; the development of tools; and the testing and evaluation of tools. Thus, for example, with respect to training, work on learning theory would feed directly into the design of specific materials, courses, learning aids and programs for experimental use in the System. These would then be subject to testing and evaluation. In the field of indicators, work on the theory of indicators (both quantitative and qualitative), would dovetail with their application by a monitoring unit, and their evaluation by a testing group. In this way, I believe, the BBL could begin to develop practical tools, the absence of which now makes it virtually impossible for the Bell System to deal effectively with its socio-cultural environment. It goes without saying that these tools have direct economic implications and that they must be adequately integrated with the economic measures and tools now used by the System.

It is also clear, however, that it is no longer possible to deal with economic matters in a socio-cultural vacuum. The creation of such a facility now could vastly simplify the corporation's conversion to a Super-Industrial form. Indeed, as the dislocations of the next few decades increase in amplitude, the social and behavioral tools developed by the BBL could well prove to be critical to the System's survival.

Summary: The proposed temporary goal for the Bell System, calling for the spinning off of certain functions now performed intramurally, and the creation, simultaneously, of a Constellation of related companies and organizations, demands the strengthening of what are here called the Framework functions.

Were these recommendations to be carried out, the result would be a two-levelled Bell System: an overarching Framework Organization to which a series of modular components are attached. These modular components correspond, in form, to what are now the operating companies, Western Electric, and Bell Labs. Each of these, however, would examine its internal structure to find parts of itself, or functions, that could be equally well performed by non-Bell companies or organizations. By transferring functions to these, a ring of associated firms or organizations would be created around the Bell System, itself. Together, these—Bell and the organizations serving it—would form the Bell Communications Constellation.

To assure that high standards are met throughout the System, with regard not merely to technical specifications, but to economic and social performance, the Framework Organization would be dramatically strengthened. The Framework Organization would provide assistance to both the Bell modules and to the other organizations in the Constellation—especially in the fields of quality control, manpower development, environment, regulatory matters, and planning. A major addition would be the creation of the Bell Behavioral Laboratories to serve as an extra support unit for the whole Constellation.

Chapter 12

Epilogue

COMMENTARY:

It is always easier to talk about change than to make it. It is easier to consult than to manage. In writing this report, I tried never to lose sight of these simple truths. No matter how detailed or complex, our descriptions of organizational reality are always over-simplified. And no matter how clear a proposed strategy, it can never be executed as written. Unless it is designed, communicated and implemented in real time, it must, of necessity, be fading into obsolescence even as it is read. What is more, even the best strategies seldom take into account more than a few of the consequences that flow from them. In real life, the decision-maker must continually adjust to those consequences, and, in doing so, deviate from the clear course laid out in advance.

Despite all these objections, however, a corporation without a strategy is like an airplane weaving through stormy skies, hurled up and down, slammed by the wind, lost in the thunderheads. If lightning or crushing winds don't destroy it, it will simply run out of gas. Without some explicit assumptions about the long-range future, and strategic guidelines for dealing with them, without a vision of its own future form, even the largest and seemingly most secure organizations face disaster in a period of revolutionary, technological and economic turbulence.

These are some of the considerations that went into the preparation of this document for the Bell System. And if there are lessons for others, they flow from the shared need to invent a more resilient, more responsive, more flexible form of business organization: The Adaptive Corporation.

REPORT:

The problems of the Bell System today are intimately connected with the social problems of the society as a whole as it begins the historic transition that will carry it beyond Industrialism. For the Bell System, this means an enormous challenge: that of converting from a classical organization of the Industrial Era to an equally successful example of Super-Industrial organization.

Only by understanding the basic social forces changing American society today can any corporation, and especially one as large and centrally important as the Bell System, hope to adapt to Super-Industrial society as it emerges.

Over the past decade, one after another, various traditional businesses engaged in by AT&T have been eliminated or hived off or opened to competition. The decisions on which these actions were based, whether taken voluntarily or forced on the company, have been, by and large, piecemeal and implemented without reference to the larger goal of transforming Bell into the nation's leading Super-Industrial corporation.

What is proposed here is not something entirely new—Bell has been changing right along—but simply that the process be continued with conscious and coherent long-range objectives in mind.

It is impossible, of course, to "prove" that the policies here proposed are "right." What can be shown is that, if our basic model of Super-Industrialism is correct, the old-style Industrial corporation will be increasingly obsolete.

One can scarcely imagine what the Bell System would have been like today if, at the opening of America's industrialization, it had attempted to function like a Medieval Guild. In the same way, it is difficult to imagine what would happen to Bell in the future, if it tried to move forward into the Super-Industrial Era while holding on to its Industrial form.

I have attempted, therefore, to sketch, in the broadest of strokes, a picture of what a Super-Industrial Bell System might look like. I have no illusions about the difficulties of transformation. It is far easier to write about change in a corporation than to bring it about. It is always easier to be the outsider, full of general ideas, than the man on the spot who must find ways to implement them.

At the same time, I know, as we all do, that the past was not without its difficulties as well. The men of Theodore Vail's generation faced enormous handicaps and succeeded, in the end, in creating something that had never before existed. That is precisely the same challenge that faces the management of the Bell System today. On their imagination, energy, and courage to change depends the basic communications system of the nation.

Notes

1. Hendrik W. Bode, "Technological Innovation and Technical Integration in the Bell System" (Draft), September 8, 1969, pp. 68–69.
2. Interview with Author.
3. *Bell System Manual.* (New York: American Telephone and Telegraph Co., 1970, p. 504.)
4. David Ash, "The Detroit Revolution," *Esquire,* July 1966.
5. Interview with Author.
6. Bode, p. 69.
7. *Bell System Manual,* p. 202.
8. *Ibid.,* p. 702.
9. *Ibid.,* p. 103.
10. *Ibid.,* p. 902.
11. Interview with Author.
12. *Events in Telephone History.* (New York: American Telephone and Telegraph Co., October 1968, pp. xviii–xix.)
13. *Ibid.*
14. American Telephone and Telegraph, *Viewpoints on Communications Policy.* (New York: American Telephone and Telegraph Co., August 1968, Part XII [Attachment 12], p. 3.)

15. Interview with Author.
16. Interview with Author.
17. *Task Force Report,* Part V, p. 18.
18. *Ibid.,* Part VI, pp. 11–12.
19. McKinsey and Co., *A Study of Western Electric's Performance.* (New York: American Telephone and Telegraph Co., 1969, p. 228.)
20. Bode, p. 89.
21. *Ibid.*
22. *Ibid.,* pp. 84, 88.
23. Interview with Author.
24. Interview with Author; and Joseph G. Goulden, *Monopoly.* (New York: Pocket Books, 1970, p. 5.)
25. Interview with Author.
26. Interview with Author.
27. Interview with Author.
28. *Bell System Manual,* p. 1304.
29. *Ibid.*
30. *Wall Street Journal,* June 1, 1970.
31. Interview with Author.
32. *New York Times,* February 22, 1970.
33. *Ibid.*
34. Interview with Author.
35. Kurt Borchardt, *Structure and Performance of the U.S. Communications Industry.* (Boston: Harvard University Graduate School of Business Administration, 1970, pp. 49, 51.)
36. *Datamation,* January 15, 1971, p. 75.
37. John McDonald, "Getting Our Communication Satellite Off the Ground," *Fortune,* July 1972.
38. *Wall Street Journal,* October 2, 1970.
39. Charles J. Lynch, "The Battle for Data Communications," *Innovations,* #11, 1970.
40. Alfred E. Kahn, *The Economics of Regulation,* vol. II. (New York: John Wiley & Sons, 1971, p. 136.)
41. *New York Times,* January 22, 1971.
42. *Datamation,* February, 1970, p. 241.

43. Interview with Author.
44. *Wall Street Journal,* October 19, 1970.
45. Irving Kahn, "CATV . . . Leading Edge of the Broadband Revolution," *Communications News,* December 1970.
46. *Ibid.*
47. *New York Times,* August 5, 1971.
48. *New Society,* May 7, 1970.
49. *New York Times,* February 14, 1970.
50. *Time,* March 3, 1971.
51. *Ibid.,* November 30, 1971.
52. *Ibid.*
53. Myron Brenton, "21,741 Choices for a Career," *New York Times Magazine,* October 25, 1970.
54. U.S. Department of Commerce, Bureau of the Census, *Statistical Abstract of the United States: 1971.* (Washington: Government Printing Office, 1972, p. 320.)
55. *Ibid.,* p. 5.
56. *New York Times,* March 10, 1971.
57. *Task Force Report,* Part V, p. 6.
58. *Ibid.*
59. *Ibid.,* Part V, p. 19.
60. *Ibid.,* Part VI, p. 48.
61. *Ibid.,* Part V, p. 20.
62. *Ibid.,* Part VI, p. 25.
63. H. I. Romnes, "Remarks to Annual Meeting of Shareholders," Atlanta, April 16, 1968.
64. "Why You Hear a Busy Signal at AT&T," *Business Week,* December 27, 1969.
65. Interview with Author.
66. *Bell System Manual,* pp. 712, 716–17.
67. McKinsey, p. 210.
68. Shirley Katzander, "New York Tel's Information Gap," *New York,* August 25, 1969.
69. *Wall Street Journal,* December 14, 1970.
70. American Telephone and Telegraph Co., Department of Environmental Affairs, "A Method of Labor Market Esti-

mation,'' in *Annual Report*. (New York: American Telephone and Telegraph Co., 1970, p. 1.)

71. W. W. Straley, remarks before the American College Public Relations Association, Denver, July 7, 1970, in *ibid.,* p. 6.
72. ''The 500 Largest U.S. Industrial Corporations,'' *Fortune,* May 1972.
73. *New York Times,* March 21, 1971, October 18, 1971.
74. *Events in Telephone History,* p. 52.
75. *Ibid.,* p. 61.
76. *New York Times,* August 16, 1969.
77. Alfred Kahn, vol. II, p. 29.
78. *Wall Street Journal,* December 11, 1970.
79. *Ibid.,* June 29, 1971.
80. *Datamation,* October 1, 1971.
81. *New York Times,* March 21, 1971, sec. 2.
82. *Wall Street Journal,* January 4, 1971.
83. Ron Rosenbaum, ''Secrets of the Little Blue Box,'' *Esquire,* October 1971.
84. Joseph Goulden and Marshall Singer, ''Dial-A-Bomb: AT&T and the ABM,'' *Ramparts,* November 1969.
85. Abbie Hoffman, *Steal This Book.* (New York: Grove Press, 1971, pp. 75ff.)
86. *New York Times,* July 7, 1970.
87. *Wall Street Journal,* September 23, 1971.
88. *Business Week,* December 27, 1969.
89. *New York Times,* July 29, 1969.
90. Interview with Author.
91. Interview with Author.
92. Donella H. Meadows, Dennis L. Meadows, Jorgen Randers, William W. Behrens III, *The Limits to Growth.* (New York: Universe Books, 1972.)
93. ''Economic Growth: New Doubts About an Old Idea,'' *Time,* March 2, 1970.
94. See above, pp. 33–35.
95. Interview with Author.

96. "A Large Question About Large Corporations," *Fortune,* May 1972.
97. McKinsey, p. 63.
98. *Ibid.,* p. 64.
99. *Ibid.*
100. *United States of America v. Western Electric Company Inc., and American Telephone and Telegraph Co.,* Final Judgment, Civil Action No. 17–49, U.S. District Court, District of N.J., January 24, 1956.
101. Interview with Author.
102. Interview with Author.
103. Henry M. Boettinger, "A Suggestion Toward Controlled Evolution of the Bell System," April 7, 1970.
104. Interview with Author.
105. Paul J. Garfield and Wallace Lovejoy, *Public Utility Economics.* (Englewood Cliffs, N.J.: Prentice-Hall, 1964, pp. 447–48.)
106. "Work When You Want To: An Idea Whose Time Has Come," *Europa Magazine,* April 1972.
107. Interview with Author.
108. Garfield and Lovejoy, p. 56.
109. Interview with Author.
110. "Industry Rates Itself," *Business and Society Review,* Spring 1972.
111. *Ibid.*

Selected Bibliography

American Telephone and Telegraph, *Annual Reports*. (New York: American Telephone and Telegraph Co., 1940 to date.)

American Telephone and Telegraph Co., *Viewpoints on Communications Policy*. (New York: American Telephone and Telegraph, 1968.)

"Are Firms Getting Too Big to Be Efficient?," *International Management,* May 1971.

"AT&T's Age of Anxiety," *Fortune,* May 1970.

Baier, Kurt, and Rescher, Nicholas (eds.), *Values and the Future*. (New York: The Free Press, 1969.)

Baker, William O., "The Use of Computers in Communications Systems," ISA *Transactions,* vol. 6, 1965.

Baran, Paul, "The Future Computer Utility," *The Public Interest,* Summer 1967.

Baran, Paul, *Notes on Seminar on Future Broad-Band Communications*. (Middletown, Conn.: Institute for the Future, February 1970.)

Bauer, Raymond (ed.), *Social Indicators*. (Cambridge: The M.I.T. Press, 1966.)

Beer, Stafford, *Decision and Control*. (New York: John Wiley & Sons, 1966.)

The Bell System and the City, November 1968.
Bell System Manual. (New York: American Telephone and Telegraph Co., 1970.)
Bennis, Warren G., *Changing Organizations.* (New York: McGraw-Hill, 1966.)
Birnbaum, Norman, *The Crisis of Industrial Society.* (New York: Oxford University Press, 1969.)
Blau, Peter M., *Bureaucracy in Modern Society.* (New York: Random House, 1956.)
Blau, Peter M., and Scott, Richard W., *Formal Organizations.* (San Francisco: Chandler Publishing Co., 1962.)
Bode, H. W., "Technological Innovation and Technical Integration in the Bell System," Draft Report, September 8, 1969.
Boettinger, Henry M., *Moving Mountains.* (New York: The Macmillan Co., 1969.)
Boettinger, H. M., *Some Aspects of Management and Technology.* (New York: American Telephone and Telegraph Co., 1970.)
Borchardt, Kurt, *Structure and Performance of the U.S. Communications Industry.* (Boston: Harvard University Graduate School of Business Administration, 1970.)
Boulding, Kenneth, *The Meaning of the Twentieth Century.* (New York: Harper & Row, 1964.)
Boulding, Kenneth, *The Organizational Revolution.* (New York: Harper and Bros., 1953.)
Brooks, Harvey, *Can Science Be Planned?* (Cambridge: Harvard University Program on Technology and Society [Reprint #3], n.d.)
Brzezinski, Zbigniew, *Between Two Ages: America's Role in the Technetronic Era.* (New York: The Viking Press, 1970.)
Burck, Gilbert, "Is AT&T Playing It Too Safe?," *Fortune,* September 1960.
Calder, Nigel (ed.), *The World in 1984,* 2 vols. (Baltimore: Penguin Books, Inc., 1965.)
Cary, William L., *Politics and the Regulatory Agencies.* (New York: McGraw-Hill Book Co., 1967.)
Chase, Stuart, *The Most Probable World.* (New York: Pelican Books, 1969.)

Clark, John Maurice, *Studies in the Economics of Overhead Costs*. (Chicago: The University of Chicago Press, 1923.)

Cordtz, Dan, "The Coming Shake-Up in Telecommunications," *Fortune,* April 1970.

Crowley, Thomas H., Harris, Gerard G., Miller, Stewart E., Pierce, John R., Runyon, John P., *Modern Communications*. (New York: Columbia University Press, 1962.)

Dale, Ernest, *The Great Organizers*. (New York: McGraw-Hill Book Co., 1960.)

DeButts, John D., "The Management of Complexity," speech before the Industrial College of the Armed Forces, Washington, D.C., August 24, 1971.

Dunstan, Mary Jane, and Garlin, Patricia W., *Worlds in the Making*. (Englewood Cliffs, N.J.: Prentice-Hall, 1970.)

Events in Telephone History. (New York: American Telephone and Telegraph Co., 1969.)

Ewald, William R., Jr. (ed.), *Environment for Man: The Next Fifty Years*. (Bloomington: Indiana University Press, 1967.)

Fisk, James B., "Bell Telephone Laboratories." Reprinted from Sir John Cockcroft (ed.), *The Organization of Research Establishments*. (London: Cambridge University Press, 1965.)

Ford, Robert N., "The Art of Reshaping Jobs," *Bell Telephone Magazine,* September–October 1968.

Garfield, Paul J., and Lovejoy, Wallace F., *Public Utility Economics*. (Englewood Cliffs, N.J.: Prentice-Hall, Inc., 1964.)

General Electric, *Developing Trends and Changing Institutions: Our Future Business Environment*. (New York: General Electric [ERM-85], April 1968.

Glover, John D., and Vancil, Richard F., *Management of Transformation*. (New York: IBM, 1968.)

Goldhamer, Herbert, *The Social Effects of Communication Technology*. (New York: Russell Sage Foundation, 1970.)

Gordon, T. S., and Shef, Arthur, *National Programs and the Progress of Technological Societies*. (Washington: The American Astronomical Society, March 4–5, 1968.)

Goulden, Joseph G., *Monopoly*. (New York: Pocket Books, 1970.)

Gross, Bertram (ed.), *A Great Society?* (New York: Basic Books, Inc., 1966.)

Gross, Bertram, *The Managing of Organizations,* 2 vols. (Glencoe: The Free Press, 1962.)

"Growth in Demand for Communications Services," American Telephone and Telegraph, Analytical Support Center Memorandum #105, October 20, 1967.

Hart, R. I., "Needs Research," *Futures,* September 1969.

Harvard University Program on Technology and Society, *Technology and the Individual.* (Cambridge: Harvard University Program on Technology and Society, 1970.)

Havelock, Ronald G., *Planning for Innovation Through Dissemination and Utilization of Knowledge.* (Ann Arbor: Center for Research on Utilization of Scientific Knowledge, Institute for Social Research, University of Michigan, 1971.)

Hayashi, Yujiro (ed.), *Perspectives on Postindustrial Society.* (Tokyo: University of Tokyo Press, 1970.)

Helmer, Olaf, *Social Technology.* (New York: Basic Books, 1966.)

International Telecommunications Union, *From Semaphore to Satellite.* (Geneva: International Telecommunications Union, 1965.)

Jantsch, E., *Perspectives of Planning.* (Paris: OECD, 1969.)

Jantsch, E., *Technological Forecasting in Perspective.* (Paris: OECD, 1966.)

Johnson, Arno H., Jones, Gilbert E., and Lucas, Daniel B., *The American Market of the Future.* (New York: New York University Press, 1966.)

Johnson, Leland J., "The Future of Cable Television: Some Problems of Federal Regulation." (Santa Monica: The Rand Corporation [Memorandum RM-6199-FF], January 1970.)

Kahn, Alfred J., *The Economics of Regulation,* 2 vols. (New York: John Wiley & Sons, Inc., 1971.)

Kahn, Alfred J., *Studies in Social Policy and Planning.* (New York: Russell Sage Foundation, 1969.)

Kahn, Alfred J., *Theory and Practice of Social Planning.* (New York: Russell Sage Foundation, 1969.)

Kahn, Herman, and Weiner, Anthony, *The Year 2000*. (New York: The Macmillan Co., 1967.)

Katz, Milton, *The Function of Tort Liability in Technology Assessment*. (Cambridge: Harvard University, Program on Technology and Society [Reprint #9], n.d.)

Katzander, Shirley, "New York Tel's Information Gap," *New York,* August 25, 1969.

Lilly, Robert, "The Social Problems of the Day." (New York: American Telephone and Telegraph Co., September 1970.)

Lynch, Charles J., "The Battle for Data Communications," *Innovations,* no. 11, 1970.

Maddox, Brenda, *Beyond Babel: New Directions in Communications*. (London: Andre Deutsch, 1972.)

Marris, Robin, *The Economic Theory of 'Managerial' Capitalism*. (London: Macmillan, 1964.)

Martin, James, *Telecommunications and the Computer*. (Englewood Cliffs, N.J.: Prentice-Hall, Inc., 1969.)

Mason, Otis T., *The Origins of Invention*. (Cambridge: The M.I.T. Press, 1966.)

Mathieson, Stuart L., and Walker, Phillip, *Computers and Telecommunications: Issues in Public Policy*. (Englewood Cliffs, N.J.: Prentice-Hall, 1970.)

Mayo, Louis H., *Comments on Senate Resolution 78*. (Washington: Program of Policy Studies in Science and Technology, George Washington University, March 4, 1969.)

Mayo, Louis H., *The Technology Assessment Function*. (Washington: Program of Policy Studies in Science and Technology, George Washington University, July 1968.)

Mayo, Louis H., and Lakshmikanth, Rao, Penna, *The Technology Assessment Function: Illustrative Cases of the Assessment of Technological Applications*. (Washington: Program of Policy Studies in Science and Technology, George Washington University, July 1968.)

McGee, John S., *In Defense of Industrial Concentration*. (New York: Praeger Publishers, 1971.)

McKinsey and Co., *A Study of Western Electric's Performance*. (New York: American Telephone and Telegraph Co., 1969.)

McMains, Harvey J., "The Socio-Economic Aspects of the Bell System Network," speech before the Economics of Regulated Public Utilities Symposium, Chicago, June 22–27, 1969.

McMains, Harvey J., *Wideband Communications: A Long-Range Study*. (New York: American Telephone and Telegraph Co., December 1965.)

McWhirter, William A., "What Hath God Rung?," *Life,* December 12, 1969.

Meadows, Donella H., Meadows, Dennis L., Randers, Jorgen, Behrens, William W. III, *The Limits to Growth*. (New York: Universe Books, 1972.)

Meier, R. L., "Tokyo: Creating Japan's Information Industry," unpublished paper, October 1969.

Mesthene, Emmanuel G., "How Technology Will Shape the Future," *Science,* July 12, 1968.

Moonman, Eric (ed.), *Science and Technology in Europe*. (Baltimore: Penguin Books, Inc., 1968.)

National Academy of Sciences, *Technology: Processes of Assessment and Choice*. (Washington: Government Printing Office, July 1969.)

National Commission on Technology, Automation and Economic Progress, *Technology and the American Economy*. (Washington: Government Printing Office, February 1966.)

National Goals Research Staff, *Toward Balanced Growth: Quantity with Quality*. (Washington, D.C.: Government Printing Office, 1970.)

National Industrial Conference Board, *The Challenge of Technology*. (New York: National Industrial Conference Board, November 30, 1966.)

New Republic, The (eds.), *America Tomorrow: Creating the Great Society*. (New York: Signet, 1965.)

"100 Years of Progress: The Bell System Telephone Set," *The Western Electric Engineer,* vol. 13, January 1969.

"100 Years of Progress: Bell System Switching Equipment," *The Western Electric Engineer,* vol. 13, April 1969.

Ozbekhan, Hasan, *Technology and Man's Future*. (Santa Monica: System Development Corporation, May 27, 1966.)

Ozbekhan, Hasan, *The Triumph of Technology: "Can" Implies "Ought."* (Santa Monica: System Development Corporation, June 6, 1967.)

Palisi, Bartolomeo, "Some Suggestions About the Transitory-Permanence Dimension of Organizations," *The British Journal of Sociology,* June 1970.

Polak, Fred L., *The Image of the Future,* 2 vols. (New York: Oceana Publications, 1961.)

Polak, Fred L., *Prognostics.* (New York: Elsevier Publishing Co., 1971.)

President's Commission on National Goals, *Goals for Americans.* (New York: The American Assembly, 1960.)

Questions and Answers on Current Issues. (New York: American Telephone and Telegraph Co., Information Department, November 1968.)

Reinhold, Budd, "The Dallas Traffic Work Itself Trial," speech before the Bell System Vice President–Personnel Conference, March 1970.

Report on Training Experience: Bell System—Plant Department. (New York: American Telephone and Telegraph Co., Operations Department and Safety Training and Organization Section, 1970.)

"The Revolution in the Phone Business," *Business Week,* November 6, 1971.

Robinson, E. A. G., *The Structure of Competitive Industry.* (Chicago: University of Chicago Press, 1957.)

Romnes, H. I., "Communications in a Changing World," speech before General Assembly Meeting, Telephone Pioneers of America, September 18, 1968.

Romnes, H. I., "Remarks Before the New York Society of Security Analysts." (New York: American Telephone and Telegraph Co., February 13, 1968.)

Romnes, H. I., "The Role of Business in Community Development," H. Chase Stone Lecture, The Colorado College, November 21, 1968.

Shanks, Michael, *The Innovators.* (New York: Penguin Books, Inc., 1967.)

Sheldon, Eleanor B., and Moore, Wilbert E., *Indicators of Social Change*. (New York: Russell Sage Foundation, 1968.)

Sloan Commission on Cable Communications, *On the Cable: The Television of Abundance*. (New York: McGraw-Hill Book Co., 1971.)

Stanford Research Institute, *The World of 1975*. (San Francisco: Stanford Research Institute, 1964.)

Stigler, George J., *The Organization of Industry*. (Illinois: Richard D. Irwin, Inc., 1968.)

Technology and Values. (Cambridge: Harvard University Program on Technology and Society [Research Review #3], Spring 1969.)

Telephone's $3 Billion Landmark in Corporate Financing. (New York: The Bond Buyer, 1970.)

Toffler, Alvin, *Future Shock*. (New York: Random House, 1970.)

Toffler, Alvin (ed.), *The Futurists*. (New York: Random House, 1972.)

"Toward the Year 2000: Work in Progress," *Daedalus,* Summer 1967.

U.S. Department of Health, Education and Welfare, *Toward a Social Report*. (Washington: Government Printing Office, 1969.)

Urban, G. R., *Can We Survive Our Future?* (London: The Bodley Head, 1972.)

Western Electric, *Annual Reports*. (New York: American Telephone and Telegraph Co., 1940 to date.)

"Why Nothing Seems to Work Any More," *Time,* March 23, 1970.

Wittenbert, F. R., "Bigness vs. Profitability," *Harvard Business Review,* January 1970.

Wollan, Michael, *Controlling the Potential Hazards of Government-Sponsored Technology*. (Washington: Program of Policy Studies in Science and Technology, George Washington University [Reprint #2], November 1968.

Zwicky, Fritz, *Discovery, Invention, Research.* (New York: The Macmillan Co., 1969.)

Appendix A:

Alternative Strategies for Public Participation

ON PARTICIPATION

In return for wage and other concessions, some U.S. labor unions have recently won agreements to participate in a limited way in making decisions previously regarded as management's sole prerogative. In addition, at the shop floor level, many large firms have begun to experiment with employee participation—although the decisions seldom involve such crucial issues as investment or new products.

American multinational corporations have also felt rising pressures for worker participation in Europe, where Sweden has set up union-controlled investment funds fed by tax revenues, and in the E.E.C., which has been debating new regulations that would compel companies to disclose to their unions information previously regarded as belonging to management—data on plant closings, take-overs, etc.

As the effects of deregulation accumulate, it is likely that many American companies will feel increasing pressure, too. But this pressure will not just come from unions. It will, I believe, arise from many other constituencies as well—including customers.

I believe that the entire issue of broadened participation in corporate decision-making needs more imaginative treatment than it has until now received, and that there is justification for public involvement in certain corporate decision-making processes on the grounds of both efficiency and equity. Rather than viewing these pressures as negative, therefore, I proposed a novel program to link public participation with the planning process.

Some will no doubt regard this proposal as utopian and unrealistic. But it is important to remember a crucial fact: AT&T was a private company, but it was also far more than that. It was—indeed, still is—a public institution, whose decisions on investment, product and other issues have a massive impact on the nation.

Pressures for public participation in corporate policy-making, or for new mechanisms to ensure social responsibility by the corporation, are likely to grow more intense in the years immediately ahead. Even if Ralph Nader retired and the present anti-business mood in the nation were to evaporate overnight, these pressures would continue to mount.

High visibility corporations like AT&T will come under special attack. One can visualize, for example, a presidential candidate in 1972 or 1976 capitalizing on the difficulties of AT&T and making its problems a campaign issue.

Nor are these pressures directly related to AT&T's "service" difficulties. Even if all telephones were functioning perfectly, AT&T would still be the target of severe criticism focussed on problems arising from pollution, ghetto employment, military contracting, etc.

> The Corporation can ignore these attacks.
>
> The Corporation can deal with them tactically, via public relations gestures.
>
> The Corporation can commit itself to radical changes without advance opportunity to assess their consequences.
>
> The Corporation can commit itself to substantive changes, insisting, however, on the need to test such changes on a pilot basis beforehand.

This memorandum assumes that the pressures for corporate responsibility and public participation are not primarily the result of anti-business "troublemaking" by dissidents, but arise from deep-seated changes in the society. For this reason, I believe that any attempt to ignore the problem or to paper over it with empty gestures would not only fail, but boomerang—causing the Corporation unnecessary harassment and danger.

It is a serious mistake to see the participatory thrust only in terms of a threat to managerial prerogative.

In fact, properly organized forms of participation represent not a threat, but a partial solution to problems that, over the long run, threaten corporate survival.

The present situation thus presents AT&T with a set of unparalleled opportunities to assert national leadership in the business community, to demonstrate corporate good faith and good citizenship, and—most important—*to improve vastly its own planning efforts and its ability to cope with accelerative change.*

EARLY WARNING SYSTEM

The key to this opportunity is the recognition that accelerative change is the single most important environmental force that any company, and especially AT&T, must learn to deal with in the decades ahead. Many of the difficulties of the company stem from its limited ability to anticipate change, to sense the warning signals that precede most major shifts in the social environment. Like most companies, it has lacked the "early warning" mechanisms made necessary by the accelerative pace of change.

I believe that "public participation" is a crucial part of any corporate early warning system, and that, unless this is recognized, AT&T and other major companies will face still greater shocks and jolts in the years immediately ahead.

In a society convulsing with change, the central need of management is for far more sensitive information—especially anticipatory information—about the environment in which the company must function. This information must go beyond economics. It is important for the corporation to know about social stresses, potential crises, shifts of population, changes in family structure, political upheavals and to know about these early enough to make adaptive decisions.

Timely information of this kind can, in the end, only come from the public, whose members are, in fact, involved in these changes. Thus in converting AT&T from a corporation grounded in Industrialism to one that is adapted to the emerging Super-Industrial society, it is of crucial importance that ways be found to tap into not merely the specific service needs of the telephone consumer, but also into the wishes, values, plans of various community groups, agencies and institutions. This can only be done with cooperation *from* these groups, agencies and institutions.

It is possible to begin work now toward the construction of an early warning system for AT&T to be based, in part, on new forms of public participation.

Moreover, I believe this can be done without racing blindly into radical policies or programs.

In the following pages I shall discuss a number of alternative public participation strategies and suggest how AT&T might break fresh ground in the corporate community.

Strategy 1: The GM Model

Creation of a special committee of the Board of Directors to concern itself with "corporate social responsibility."

This strategy increases the already serious credibility gap between business and the public. However intelligent, decent and socially conscious the members of such a committee, it will and must look like cosmetic surgery to the outside world. Philip Moore, a coordinator of the Nader-triggered Project on Corporate Responsibility, attacked the GM strategy on grounds that it is a "whitewash if corporations turn only to their own ranks to determine the public impact" of their decisions. Such a response is natural, understandable, inevitable.

Other weaknesses: The sudden creation of a new committee of the Board to worry about social responsibility is tacit admission that either no one worried about this before, or that it was not regarded as important enough to merit committee status until now.

This strategy rejects the concept of public participation, therefore not merely exacerbating the critics, but missing the opportunity to make positive use of certain forms of participation.

In addition, were AT&T to adopt the GM Model, it would appear to be a follower, rather than a leader in the business community.

Recommendation: For these reasons, I urge rejection of Strategy 1.

Strategy 2: The Public Director Model

Expansion of the present Board of Directors to include "public members."

This strategy meets the demand raised by the Project on Corporate Responsibility for wider representation on company boards. GM was criticized—with justice, in my view—for having a board that is homogeneous—all male, and all white. Most corporate boards are also homogeneous in terms of age, income, and outlook.

I believe that a Board of Directors will be more capable of serving its stockholders and the public, as well as more useful to the management, if its membership reflects diverse constituencies. But I do not believe that the problems of corporate responsibility and of participation can be solved by the ritual addition to the Board of "public members."

Such a solution often leads to one of two results: either the "public members" are co-opted and take on the coloration of the Board as a whole, so that they become virtually useless as a source of fresh inputs; or they become mechanical spokesmen for special groups whose interests coincide with neither the corporation nor the public.

This strategy also suffers from the credibility gap problem, and it does nothing to turn "participation" into a positive resource for the Corporation.

Recommendation: I regard Strategy 2 as a weak strategy—unlikely to accomplish what its proponents desire.

Strategy 3: The Advisory Board Model

Creation of an independent advisory board with powers to make public reports to the Board on the social consequences of AT&T policies.

While arming an independent advisory board with the authority to publish its findings would demonstrate corporate good faith, this strategy, by itself, also suffers from serious shortcomings.

Typically, such boards are composed of senior officials or prominent citizens who are mandated to collect and analyze data and to prepare reports which may or may not be made public.

However, those who have served on such bodies are the first to admit that their findings, as a rule, are ignored. Even when such panels are well-funded and competently staffed, even when their findings are widely publicized, their recommendations are seldom implemented.

So well known are these weaknesses, that the appointment or election of yet another advisory board is often itself taken as evidence that the company or government agency is dodging its responsibility. The credibility problem remains significant.

Recommendation: For these reasons, I regard Strategy 3 as inadequate.

I believe, however, that *there is a way for AT&T to adapt the advisory board model to its own needs, to create a wholly new kind of advisory panel—one so dramatically different that it will greatly reduce the credibility problem, one that can do more for the company than produce eloquent but unread reports.*

Strategy 4 suggests how.

Strategy 4: The Early Warning Model

Creation of an independent Council of Public Advisors with powers to issue public reports and to fund experiments in public participation.

This strategy is based on two premises.

First, the shortcomings of the typical advisory board flow from the fact that it is essentially an inert body, rather than an action agency, and from the fact that it lacks continuing contact with those, at *various* levels of the relevant system, who would have to implement its findings. So long as these remain the case, the advisory board is virtually doomed to ineffectuality.

Second, we know very little about "public participation" and we need to know more. There are many different ways to involve the public in corporate or community decision-making. But no one yet knows which way or ways are best.

Strategy 4, therefore, seeks to solve both these problems. It begins with an advisory board, but gives to it a function not ordinarily assigned to advisory boards—that of funding certain action projects. These projects are, in effect, limited-scale experiments with public participation.

The functions of the Council of Public Advisors, therefore, would be a combination of the traditional and the innovative:

- To issue periodic reports and recommendations on AT&T's social performance, encompassing such subjects as pollution, conservation, public safety, and public responsiveness.

- To provide a non-governmental forum for the public discussion of communications policy, through sponsorship of open conferences, seminars, perhaps even gaming and simulation sessions in which participants learn some of the problems of running the nation's communications system.

- To suggest company policies on emerging social issues—particularly, though not exclusively, those having implications for the communications industry—privacy, for example.

- To design, fund, and provide staff support for a variety of experiments in public participation to be carried out not at the AT&T level, but as close to the grass roots level as possible—within the associated companies.

- To evaluate these and other experiments, and to advise the Corporation on ways of achieving forms of public participation that benefit the nation's communications system.

What kinds of experiments are proposed?

I said earlier that there are many ways to involve the public in the life of a business, and that some forms of participation can produce important intelligence for those charged with managing it.

Here are some examples worth testing in carefully designed local experiments.

1. *Communications Councils*—Only recently has the federal executive recognized the need for an office reporting directly to the President on policy questions in the communications field. It is not surprising, therefore, that comparable offices do not exist in major metropolitan areas. In fact, one source of difficulty in corporate planning is inadequate liaison between business planners and responsible city and community officials. Note the absence in most cities of an agency or group that brings together, on a regular basis and in a non-adversary manner, operating managers of the Bell System, local Mayors or their representatives, city planning authorities, and consumer spokesmen.

   AT&T should encourage the formation of such Communications Councils on an experimental basis in cities of various size and even on a neighborhood basis—in Watts, for example, or Bedford Stuyvesant.

   In communities experiencing rapid transitions in communication patterns, Communications Councils could explore such questions as facilitation of installation and maintenance operations, reduction of vandalism of public phones, recruitment, training, etc. Citywide Communications Councils could consider such citywide questions as CATV policy, location of plant sites, timetables for major maintenance or installation operations, population mobility, and the potential impact of local business trends on communication needs.

Exactly how such Councils might be organized, who should participate in them, how large a jurisdiction they should serve are among the questions that cannot be answered dogmatically and in the absence of actual experience. The Council of Public Advisors ought to consider such issues in designing local experiments, and stand prepared to help local Bell System managers in carrying them out.

2. *Future User Committees*—Technological advances have diversified the communications market creating distinctive communication constituencies. As society differentiates further and technical advances proliferate, AT&T must anticipate the formation of an increasing number of specialized user groups.

   Such groups need to be seen not simply as countervailing forces, but as important sources of intelligence about forthcoming technological and business changes. Thus, rather than passively awaiting their formation—usually as a result of some joint complaint against AT&T—it may be wise to encourage their formation in fields that are still small and inchoate, but which may develop into major users in the future. Examples: ocean industries; microbiology.

   By taking a role in forming such groups, AT&T can help shape their development—and increase its intake of anticipatory intelligence.

   The Council of Public Advisors could experiment with the formation of such groups and their organization into systematic sources of valuable information for planning.

3. *Public Consultant Program*—Either on a neighborhood or a citywide basis, the local telephone company could operate a continuing program that invites randomly selected subscribers to come to the business office and spend several hours as a paid "Telephone Consultant." Interviewees would be encouraged to voice their grievances or complaints about the system, but also to indicate their willingness to absorb the cost of innovations in equipment, their acceptance of new billing procedures, pricing, etc. They could be asked about community issues, the likelihood of various changes in

the community, their own plans for future change in terms of job, residence, education, etc. Done on a neighborhood basis, such polling could give users a sense that their opinions are valued and could, at the same time, provide vital information for planners concerned with new plant and switching installations, marketing and advertising programs, forthcoming regulatory problems, looming urban difficulties.

4. *Monthly Bill Survey*—A variation of the above might be the systematic use of the monthly bill as a survey questionnaire to ascertain customer satisfaction levels, to determine attitudes toward proposed innovations, to record grievances, etc. Data collected from both the Telephone Consultant Program and the Monthly Bill Survey might prove useful not merely to planners but to those charged with representing the company before regulatory agencies.
5. *External Suggestion Program*—Many consumers believe they have valuable ideas for improving telephone service or adding new services. Whether any significant percentage of these have merit or not, a program might be designed for encouraging their submission and for rewarding participants in the program.
6. *Community Feedback Program*—A significant variation of the External Suggestion Program is a program for encouraging public suggestions for improving community services, as distinct from telephone services. A local telephone office could offer to receive public ideas for improved community services and to channel them to appropriate city agencies. Such a program has a precedent in the successful volunteer action programs now being run by many radio stations and newspapers in an attempt to establish close links with their audience.
7. *Ombudsman Program*—AT&T could extend the ombudsman concept to the quasi-public sector by recommending establishment of ombudsman offices in certain telephone districts. The financing of the ombudsman's office might be a joint effort between the operating companies and local or state governments to ensure credibility of the office.

8. *Referendum Program*—Where community disputes arise over plant location or other issues, operating companies or even districts could offer to submit alternative plans to referendum after extended public debate. (Experiments are now under way entailing use of computers in conducting continuing community referenda on environmental issues, first exposing voters to alternative statements of the problem and alternative solutions, then asking them to vote unofficially.)

Each of these programs not only provides consumers and others some opportunity to "be heard" by the company, but by the same token, produces data that, properly compiled, analyzed and presented, can help management anticipate change and make more soundly based decisions. Moreover, the kind of data produced is precisely in the social, political, values area that is, by and large, lacking in most corporate planning efforts.

It is for this reason that the entire public participation thrust needs to be seen as potentially valuable, rather than simply a threat.

The specific programs suggested above vary greatly in costs, benefits, risks, credibility, etc. This is precisely why they should *not* be undertaken on an across-the-board, corporation-wide basis, but should be examined and tested in limited trials. The Council of Public Advisors ought to have the responsibility for designing such experiments, funding them, and providing technical assistance in running them, so that the operating companies or subdivisions do not need to bear the costs by themselves.

A Council of Public Advisors that announces from the start that it does not have all the answers about public participation, but that it is seriously concerned about finding some of the answers, will have far greater credibility, both in the business community and in the larger community, than one which issues the usual rhetoric. Similarly, a Council that stands prepared to run some real-life experiments will be more respected, even for its shortcomings, than a traditional advisory panel that simply declares it will "study" the problem.

At the same time, the involvement with these local groupings, and with Bell System people at all levels of the Corporation, create for the Council both a following and a sense of reality.

If the assumption is correct that the issue of corporate responsibility and public involvement is likely to grow more, rather than less, intense, Strategy 4 makes it possible for AT&T to do something serious, substantive and creative about it.

In the absence of a Council of Public Advisors, or some similar mechanism, the issues that confront the Corporation publicly are determined in an *undemocratic* fashion. Extreme or highly unrepresentative groups are able to choose the terrain for guerilla warfare against the telephone system. The existence of a Council, democratically constituted and honestly independent, will not and should not protect the Corporation against criticism. But it can set the ground rules for debate, make the process more constructive and responsible. It can provide a vehicle for democratic discussion that simply does not now exist.

To summarize, therefore, *Strategy 4: The Early Warning Model,* provides AT&T with:

- an opportunity to strengthen corporate planning through contact with community and other groups whose policies will increasingly affect the company's future;

- an opportunity to build a new kind of management data base that will help in making or substantiating pricing, investment and capital construction decisions;

- an opportunity to identify in advance company policies that might trigger hostile response from either organized or unorganized subscribers;

- an opportunity to strengthen employee morale, restoring some of the prestige lost because of seeming failures to anticipate and resolve constituent grievances;

- an opportunity to exert national leadership.

Recommendation: For these reasons, I urge that Strategy 4 be given serious study before a decision is made.

A NOTE ON INDEPENDENCE

The independence of the Council of Public Advisors is important not merely because it is essential to credibility, but also because it is likely to increase cooperation in generating useful information for planning and early warning purposes.

The independence of the Council might be strengthened in various ways. This is not the place to evaluate all these methods, but merely to list some of them:

1. *Financial.* The Council should have a guaranteed source of financial support—not wholly dependent upon AT&T. Possible techniques for achieving this include endowment. The Council could also be given the right to receive funds from other sources under certain conditions.
2. *Membership.* The Council ought to reflect diverse constituencies. It ought to be as democratic as possible in both composition and procedures, without at the same time allowing the telephone system, a national resource, to become the political football of highly unrepresentative groups.

   The difficulties of selecting members of the Council are too complex to be dealt with in this preliminary discussion, beyond noting that the selection method is, of course, absolutely critical in establishing the independence, effectiveness and credibility of the Council. Before a decision is made, a wide range of alternative methods ought to be systematically explored.

   Whatever methods are ultimately arrived at, however, I would urge strongly that members of the Council of Public Advisors should *not* be directors or employees of AT&T or its subsidiaries. Members or employees of the Council should pledge that upon leaving they will not accept contracts from or employment in the Bell System or any organization making a grant to the Council.

3. *Publication.* The Council should have the right to publish its findings and recommendations.

Much of the work of the Council—that involving actual experimentation—cannot take place without the consent and cooperation of AT&T or its subsidiaries. In this sense, the Council cannot function properly without continuing company support. At the same time, the dignity of the Council and its power to publish provides it with a measure of independent influence.

This creates, in effect, a system of checks and balances essential to its believability and its effectiveness. Because it is not simply a blue-ribbon panel but, in part, an active enterprise whose staff and members will have continuing contact with Bell System people at all levels, it is likely to appreciate the day-to-day difficulties entailed in managing the system, and sympathize with the necessity for "early warning" information.

Hopefully, the Council would see itself not simply as a "Watchdog" or critic of the Corporation, but as an ally in sensing future problems, in designing rapport with community institutions and agencies, in helping prepare the nation's communications system for rapid change.

Appendix B:

Partial List of Individuals Consulted

Adelson, Marvin	Professor of Organization University of California, Los Angeles
Allingham, Jack	Department of Sociology University of Western Ontario
Alston, Angus	President Southwestern Bell
Baker, William O.	Vice President Bell Telephone Laboratories
Barrett, Charles	Vice President Newmeyer Associates
Benn, Anthony Wedgwood	Member of Parliament Great Britain
Blass, Walter	Director, Corporate Planning New York Telephone
Block, Edward	Assistant Vice President, Public Relations and Employee Information American Telephone and Telegraph
Bode, Hendrick W.	Professor of Engineering Harvard University
Boettinger, Henry M.	Director, Management Sciences American Telephone and Telegraph
Borwick, Richard	Vice President Newmeyer Associates
Collis, Sidney R.	Assistant Vice President, Construction Plans American Telephone and Telegraph
Cook, George	Vice President, Regulatory Matters American Telephone and Telegraph
Crossland, Edward B.	Vice President, Federal Relations American Telephone and Telegraph
DeButts, John	Chairman of the Board American Telephone and Telegraph
Dordich, Herbert	Director, Office of Telecommunications New York City Government

Dynes, Charles	Information Director, Public Relations and Employee Information American Telephone and Telegraph
Ehrlich, Robert W.	Director, Corporate Planning Studies American Telephone and Telegraph
Fisk, James B.	President Bell Telephone Laboratories, Inc.
Galli, Anthony	Vice President N. W. Ayer & Co.
Gerjuoy, Herbert	Professor of Public Administration State University of New York, Albany
Johnson, Leland	RAND Corporation
Johnson, Nicholas	Commissioner Federal Communications Commission
Kamiya, Haruo	Central Executive Center Zendentsu (Communications Workers Union)
Kobayashi, Koji	President and Chief Executive Officer Nippon Electric
Kokado, Hiroshi	Deputy Manager, Management Research Division Nippon Telephone & Telegraph Corp.
Lloyd-Jones, David	Staff Member House of Representatives, Select Subcommittee on Education
McKay, Kenneth	Vice President, Engineering American Telephone and Telegraph
McMains, Harvey	Director, Management Sciences American Telephone and Telegraph
Moulton, Horace	Vice President and General Counsel American Telephone and Telegraph
Owens, Cornelius	Executive Vice President American Telephone and Telegraph

Ozawa, Haruo	Deputy Manager, Manager, Management Research Division Nippon Telephone & Telegraph Corp.
Romnes, H. I.	Chairman of the Board (Retired) American Telephone and Telegraph
Rosoff, Peter	Director, Regulatory Research American Telephone and Telegraph
Ryan, James	Assistant Vice President, Public Relations and Employee Information American Telephone and Telegraph
Sanuki, T.	Professor Japan Development Bank, Waseda University
Simis, Theodore	Assistant Vice President, Marketing and Service Plans American Telephone and Telegraph
Singer, Ben	Professor of Sociology Dartmouth College
Straley, Walter	Vice President Deere & Co.
Tait, Lee	Vice President and General Manager The Chesapeake & Potomac Telephone Co. of Virginia
Takeda, Teruo	Manager, Management Research Division Nippon Telephone & Telegraph Corp.
Tekeuchi, Misao	Chief, Control Section, Management Research Division Nippon Telephone & Telegraph Corp.
Taylor, Phil	Assistant Vice President, Public Relations and Employee Information American Telephone and Telegraph

Thayer, Gordon	Executive Vice President, Business Information Systems Programs Bell Telephone and Telegraph
Tirone, James	Information Director, Planning; Public Relations and Employee Information American Telephone and Telegraph
Vincent, Marcel	Chairman of the Board and Chief Executive Officer Bell Canada
Von Auw, Alvin	Vice President American Telephone and Telegraph
Wells, John E.	General Marketing Manager The Pacific Telephone and Telegraph Co.
Williamson, Clifton	Assistant Vice President, Engineering American Telephone and Telegraph
Wolontis, Michael	Executive Director, Operations Research and Patents Bell Telephone Laboratories

Index

Note: Throughout these pages the names "American Telephone and Telegraph Company," "AT&T," and the "Bell System" are used interchangeably. Because they run so continuously through the text, they are not indexed, as such, although parts of the system, including Western Electric, Bell Long Lines, Bell Telephone Laboratories, and the Bell Operating Companies, are indexed. For the same reason, "telephones" and "telephony" have no specific index listing.

About the Author

Social critic and futurist Alvin Toffler's most influential works are *The Third Wave* and *Future Shock,* which won the Prix du Meilleur Livre Étranger and the McKinsey Foundation Book Award for its "distinguished contribution to management literature."

In all, his works have sold over 10 million copies in more than 30 countries. They have been cited by such political leaders as Zhao Ziyang, the Prime Minister of China, Madam Gandhi of India, Richard Nixon, and many others. They have been closely studied by top managers in the U.S. and Japan, and are routinely taught in university courses ranging from economics, planning and management to philosophy, sociology and literature.

A graduate of New York University, Mr. Toffler worked as a welder, millwright and assembly-line hand for five years before beginning his career as a journalist with an assignment to cover labor-management relations, economics and politics. After a stint as a Washington correspondent, he joined *Fortune* magazine as an Associate Editor. Later he served briefly as Visiting Professor at Cornell University, was a Visiting Scholar at the Russell Sage Foundation, and taught at the New School for Social Research. Recently named a Fellow of the American Association for the Advancement of Science, he is a much sought-after lecturer and holds honorary degrees in science, letters and law.

Mr. Toffler is married and has a grown daughter. His wife, Heidi, is his collaborator and pursues an independent career as a lecturer as well.